Citizenship and Ethnicity

**Recent Titles in
Contributions in Sociology**

CITIZENSHIP AND ETHNICITY

*The Growth and Development of
a Democratic Multiethnic Institution*

Feliks Gross

Contributions in Sociology, Number 128

GREENWOOD PRESS
Westport, Connecticut • London

Library of Congress Cataloging-in-Publication Data

Gross, Feliks, 1906–
    Citizenship and ethnicity : the growth and development of a
democratic multiethnic institution / Feliks Gross.
        p.   cm. — (Contributions in sociology, ISSN 0084–9278 ; no.
128)
    Includes bibliographical references and index.
    ISBN 0–313–30932–9 (alk. paper)
    1. Minorities.   2. State, The.   3. Ethnic relations.
4. Citizenship.   5. Nationalism.   I. Title.   II. Series.
JC312.G767   1999
323.6'09'049—dc21   99–21277

British Library Cataloguing in Publication Data is available.

Library of Congress Catalog Card Number: 99–21277
ISBN: 0–313–30932–9
ISSN: 0084–9278

First published in 1999

Greenwood Press, 88 Post Road West, Westport, CT 06881
An imprint of Greenwood Publishing Group, Inc.
www.greenwood.com

Printed in the United States of America

The paper used in this book complies with the
Permanent Paper Standard issued by the National
Information Standards Organization (Z39.48–1984).

10 9 8 7 6 5 4 3 2 1

CONTENTS

ACKNOWLEDGMENTS

This volume is a continuation—indeed a kind of second volume of a broader project—on the multiethnic state with particular attention to a civic and a tribal state. Consequently, the acknowledgments for the preceding volume, *The Civic and the Tribal State*, extend to this volume as well. I shall not list them again, but will limit myself to the few that concern this volume.

I shall again express my thanks and appreciation to Dr. James Sabin for his useful and professional advice and his suggestions. His advice to divide a large manuscript into two volumes contributes to clarity of the argument. Betty Pessagno, production editor, deserves my sincere appreciation and thanks for attention to the production of the manuscript. I thank Arlene Belzer for her thoughtful reading and careful editing.

While the subject matter has been narrowed to a single issue of development of citizenship as a multiethnic institution, the historical aspect of this subject was paramount. Thus I continued my discussions with my friend and colleague Professor Hans Trefousse, especially on the historical development of and changes in the nature of the American institution.

My thanks and words of appreciation also go to Professor Stuart Prall of the Graduate School and Queens College of the City University of New York, not only for his valuable bibliographical advice but also for his pertinent and challenging discussion of British institutions and constitutional history. I appreciate his brilliant comments and comparison to other political cultures.

I also thank Mrs. J. Sheldon for her attentive reading of proofs. My thanks also go to Dr. Kinga Galica and Dimitry Leukides for their attention and assistance in computerizing my heavily corrected, and at times, difficult typescript, as well as their interest in this work. Leukides' Hellenic comments are appreciated.

The intention of this volume is to give a short, but nevertheless valid overview, a general picture, of the continuity and fortunes of a single, but fundamental institution—citizenship—in a historical span of two millennia without making the volume a kind of historical digest or formal outline. My aim is to grasp the meaning of the totality of an institution within a specific time span and its manifold aspects and relevance as an institution of a multiethnic state. My intent is to give the reader an image of a changing but still relevant (and at times powerful) institution of changing fortunes and modifications.

This task touches on many disciplines and embraces a history of many centuries. I of course realize all the difficulties and risks of error in making facile generalizations.

This venture calls upon studies that have already covered time spans of a historical stage, a consistent historical period, and studies of the history of the institutions of a nation. What was needed was a kind of "intermediary" study, intermediary in general approach, and concerned with an extensive time span.

Some fundamental and innovating scholarly works on the history of citizenship have already been written during the last few decades. They were very helpful, even essential, in my work. I have quoted from those studies, and here I express my appreciation.

I shall list only a few and begin with the comprehensive, highly informative, and illuminating volume of Peter Riesenberg, which surveys the development of the very concept and philosophy of citizenship in a time span of two millennia, from Plato to Rousseau. This volume, *Citizenship in the Western Tradition: From Plato to Rousseau*, deserves to be a standard text in college curricula or at least required reading.

To the group of historical books that cover various aspects of citizenship in a short and definite period of time belongs an equally informative volume written by a group of scholars and published under the editorship of Renée Waldinger, Philip Dawson, and Isser Woloch—*The French Revolution and Meaning of Citizenship*. Various disciplines were applied to describe this major and symbolic institution and to project a totality of the impact of an institution within a single historical period.

Equally relevant to my work were, of course, specific studies of citizenship within a single nation or within the same state. I found the following titles not only highly informative but also fascinating reading for their rediscovery of the past: Philip B. Manville's *The Origins of Citizenship in Ancient Athens*; David Whitehead's study *The Demes of Athens*,

508–ca 250 B.C.; A. N. Sherwin-White's book *The Roman Citizenship*. Included, of course, is Aristotle's never aging *Politics*, with chapters on citizenship with instructive and penetrating comments by Ernest Barker.

The above are only a few examples of a never ending list of studies. Major contributors to this field of history and Roman law are Rudolf von Ihering ("Entwicklungs Geschichte des Römischen Rechts" in *Der Geist des Rechts. Ein Auswahl aus Seinen Schriften* edited by Fritz Buchwald), Theodor Mommsen (*The History of Rome*), Fustel de Coulanges (*La Cité Antique*)—of the older generation—and Geza Alfoldy's *Social History of Rome*—a contemporary work. Similar types of work on contemporary citizenship have also been consulted, such as James T. Kettner's *The Development of American Citizenship* and Roger Brubaker's *Citizenship and Nationhood in France and Germany*.

These are only *some* examples of the research and studies that were helpful and essential for this work, and I would like to acknowledge my appreciation. The past century was a time of great scholarship and basic research, most of which is considered too easily "dated." I have found these works illuminating and wish to acknowledge their contribution to my own scholarship.

INTRODUCTION

The way states are built often determines their future. Constructing a new polity involves building a complex political organization. In the past those ways were often simple, brutal, and cruel. The social technique tells us not only how things were done and how they work, but also what kind of institutions and structures were needed to build a state.

Unlike those states that were based in violence and coercion, and initially organized through submission, other states existed where citizenship was a major institution, an "instrument" uniting in a common polity, a shared home, diverse nationalities and racial, religious and ethnic groups. It is and was a political and social instrument in construction of a modern, democratic and multiethnic state.

The term *citizen* involves diverse concepts or definitions, but this book concerns itself with the term in the sense of democratic citizenship. This citizenship extends human, political and civil rights to all inhabitants, regardless of race, religion, ethnicity, or culture. In a civic state, which is based on the concept of such citizenship, even foreigners are protected by the rule of law.

Citizenship reflects a major dilemma of democracy: it touches on the relationship between an individual and society, between an individual and the state, and, hence, between the collective and the individual. The history of the human struggle for freedom is reflected in this dialectical issue, in search for a workable and just balance between those two components of society.

The modern democratic state provides ample ways to achieve a proper balance between those two spheres—the individual and collective, the public and the private. Extension of the public sphere increases the power and authority of the state, while limiting the private one, an area of individual freedom. This relationship is not necessarily as simple or as "certain" as a mathematical equation or game theory. The very protection of the individual as well as the extension of social rights necessitates state action and intervention.

This issue of a proper balance between the state and the individual is embodied in a political definition of citizenship. For citizenship regulates the relationship between the individual and state. The authority of the state is expressed in the citizen's duties and responsibilities, whereas civil and political rights define the freedom of an individual and set the limits of the public authority.

Citizenship in our history was a major institution in building a modern, democratic and multiethnic state. In the past, it was a major device in the development of a universal empire, inhabited by diverse peoples: the Roman Empire. This aspect of citizenship is a major theme of this volume.

Because of modern economic development, the postindustrial and global economy, and other factors, the demography of states that were at one time ethnically more homogeneous and far less diverse than today has changed. Today a demographic revolution has affected almost all of Europe. Nonimmigrant countries like Germany today have more than 3.5 million nonnationals, immigrants or their families, of which 65 percent are Yugoslavs and Turks. France has a total of 2.5 million non–European Union immigrants, 65 percent of which are North Africans. Great Britain has more than 1 million. European Union nations today have 16 million non-European immigrants.

The United States is an immigrant state, but even here the demography has changed considerably when compared with the past. The ethnic mix is different. The once European immigrants have been largely displaced by Asian, African, Caribbean and Spanish American arrivals. Today it seems that cultural differences are wider than those of earlier immigration waves. Similar changes have affected Australia and other countries as well.

The building of a modern, democratic, and this time multiethnic, multicultural state became vital. And here again, not unlike ancient Rome, citizenship is a major "instrument," a basic institution.

A multiethnic state founded on the principles of democracy is a "civic one" when it is an association of citizens, irrespective of their religion, ethnicity or race. It is not an association of members of a tribe, of a common descent people, or peoples of a common race and religion. Here ethnicity, not unlike religion, is separated from political identity.

The United States is a civic state. During the latter part of our century the United States created an efficient, pluralistic and civic system that extended equal rights to all citizens, irrespective of race, ethnicity and religion in one large, continental nation of many diverse ethnic and cultural groups. It can be considered as a model of a modern civic and democratic state. The state does not practice discrimination, although prejudice may and does survive.

This country arrived at a full civic system after a long historical journey and many struggles, a century after the Civil War, the War between the States and the abolition of slavery. This change has been expressed again in the very meaning and social, political and legal definition of the institution of citizenship. Citizenship and its meaning, as in ancient Rome, is the legal and political shield of a free person.

Since the dawn of civilization diverse ethnic groups have been tied together into a single complex polity by means of war and conquest. The defeated were forced into subject status, sometimes into bondage. Uniting differing ethnic groups by consensus, as equals, without discrimination by the "others," calls for different techniques and different principles. Such an association of different peoples, ethnic groups with equal rights for all, free of discrimination by public authorities, necessitates the need for a common bond that would embrace all, a broad bond, and in the hierarchy of accepted standards, one that rises above ethnic or racial identification; in a word, a common denominator for all. Citizenship is such a bond, it is also a vital common denominator.

The concept of citizenship means a direct association not of groups or corporations but of an individual—a person with the state. Hence, in a civic, multiethnic state a person has two identities: particular and universal. A particular identity is his ethnic self, the one he shares with his ethnic or cultural group. The universal one is citizenship—his identification with the nation-state—that is common to all members of the state, peoples of all diverse ethnic, religious or cultural groups.

In a nationalistic state all identities are fused into one. Thus, in the Croat tribal, nationalist and totalitarian state of the last war, full members of the "Ustasha Croat State" were totally "ethnic" Croats, Roman Catholics and party members. This followed, of course, the general Nazi-German model.

In a tribal state those who are "different" belong to "other" ethnic, religious or racial groups, not to the dominant cluster, and are an "out-group," subject to discrimination of varying degrees. In a democratic civic state separation of identities is a technique of uniting different cultural, ethnic and racial groups. The separation of church and state was a major step in that direction.

A pluralistic, civic system works well in today's United States and in various degrees in many countries, and in a more narrow sense in Switzerland. In contrast to the civic state, which may serve as a model for a multiethnic state, the nationalistic state, especially in its tribal form, is coercive and organized on principles of discrimination and subordination of minorities.

We shall discuss the long history in the development of the institution of citizenship as a major device in integrating a multiethnic state. This record indeed stretches from ancient Greece and Rome to modern times, a two and a half millennia chronicle. It is a history of the continuation of a single institution. Citizenship continued after the Fall of Rome in many cities of Europe and has not only been revived, but also in the eighteenth century became a symbol of a new democratic order in the United States and France. Citizenship was soon adopted by other democracies. This historical road also marks the continuity and unity of what we call today Western Civilization. It is a difficult and arduous road of struggles, confrontations and equally relevant parliamentary debates.

The preceding volume—*The Civic and the Tribal State: The State, Ethnicity, and the Multiethnic State*—has been devoted to various types of multiethnic states, primarily to the two representative and opposing ideas: the civic one and the extreme, nationalistic tribal state.

The theme of this volume is citizenship as a basic institution in construction of a democratic, multiethnic state. Citizenship however is only an articulation of the state and of the entire political culture, thus it has to be considered within the context of the state. It is necessary to introduce the major themes of this volume by citing a short survey of various types of multiethnic states and discussing the nature of a civic, pluralistic state.

The study narrowed down to a single institution—a key institution that defines an entire system and contributes to the understanding of its major functions. The meaning and relevance of the relationship between the individual and the state appears in a centuries long political and social overview that permits the reader to follow this uninterrupted continuity of an evolution, that is however not always on a hopeful or unopposed path of progress.

An attempt is made in this volume to present such a broad historical perspective. Various types of multiethnic states are briefly surveyed in the first chapter. A general outline is also given. The subject matter is vast, condensed in a short volume, hence this type of an introductory chapter serves also as a kind of general guide. In consequence, some repetitions were needed.

The field I have tried to cover is far-reaching and difficult. Alfred North Whitehead wrote that those who are afraid of errors are not prone to advance any research. A project such as this, that covers a time span of twenty-five hundred years, cannot avoid risks of error in facts and inference.

1

THE MULTIETHNIC STATE: THE WAY IT BEGAN

I

With the dynamic economic development of the post industrial era the ethnic landscape has greatly changed. Not only the American immigrant states, but also the West European have large minorities of immigrants, that differ at times strongly, in culture, religion, race and above all in language. Large minority communities, concentrated in urban areas, common at one time in Central and Eastern Europe, appeared rather suddenly in Western Europe, in France, Germany and Great Britain.

Moreover, small ethnic groups, "microethnics," survivals of ancient nationalities, leftovers of ancient wars and historical mass migrations, reappeared as active and vocal political movements. Those historical "microethnics" revitalized the quest for full recognition and identity.

All, or almost all European states had some minority groups. Now, however, with a large influx of new immigrants, differing strongly in culture, highly visible in sections of industrial cities, this issue became important and ethnic tensions made them in some cases explosive. Ethnic tensions, whatever the causes, reappeared at times with unusual vehemence and cruelty, as in Yugoslavia or in Africa, against all our hopes and pledges that after tragedies of genocides and holocaust this would not happen again.

In the past, as well as at present, some nations built democratic states where ethnic and religious groups of general cultural minorities had a rightful position, as well as all the benefits of broad toleration, often tantamount (or almost tantamount) to full equality with the personal rights enjoyed by the citizen of the dominant nation. In some other nations, often in spite of written constitutions, minorities were discriminated against in public policies as well as in everyday life.

Today, the political situation of an individual, a member of a minority or majority, is articulated in citizenship. The nature of citizenship (citizenship that is really practiced in daily life and not solely written into legal texts) also expresses the entire political system. It is an indicator of individual rights and freedom. This single institution epitomizes the modern democratic state as well as the position of the individual within the state, his human, civil and political rights as well as his duties. It is an ancient institution whose full development took more than two and a half millennia. Where can we find the beginnings of citizenship and of those democratic and humane states?

II

An attempt to identify the very beginnings—the roots so to speak—and then trace their development is still relevant. Some tribes and nations created oppressive political systems and others evolved in a different way. The historical route that shaped the definition of modern democratic citizenship is relevant indeed.

Social and political processes offer to a decision maker several choices, but at times only difficult options or alternatives are open. Once the decision or a spontaneous choice has been made, the direction of future development has been set and the return to the initial point or even change is difficult, sometimes impossible.

Construction of a state, or what we call today nation building, is an ancient art, a kind of a social political technique. Some of the historical patterns of a multiethnic state, a state of a variety of tribes, ethnic groups or nationalities, were rather simple and repetitive. It was conquest and subjugation of the weaker tribes; the defeated were always at the mercy of the victors.

The construction of the state at its very historical or prehistorical beginnings sets the direction of its development. Moreover, this decides the position and in consequence the fate of an individual, a subject or a citizen.

Powerful and large Asiatic despotic states were created this way. Once power was consolidated, tradition and lore, religion and custom, created an ideological "superstructure," which next to physical power and manipulation and fear, held together a multiethnic state. Similarly, many contemporary European states originated in conquest. But roads chosen to consolidate power were in some cases different and led to different political systems. Neither force nor conquest however were the only ways of state formation or consolidation of power.

Once the choice of a political structure had been made and a historical direction of future development set, it was indeed very difficult to change the course of history. New institutions were built, and they shaped attitudes and values. As political and economic interests of groups and individuals appeared, ruling classes were formed and affected further development and fortunes of the nascent state and its institutions. Within those conditions, created not by nature but by man and his actions, his ideas and interests, the future forms of the state of the society were later shaped.

Of course, those very beginnings affected the future. In a multiethnic community those beginnings may set a direction toward a tolerant system that later would grant equal rights to those who spoke a different language and worshipped in a different church. Other communities may prolong subjugation and serfdom.

Today, of course, "nation building" is different, although the ancient past stamps its imprint, and age-long hostilities reappear. After the two world wars states were formed with a formal blessing of a community of nations and legitimacy was usually derived from the decision and recognition of the United Nations and its member states.

The very beginning of the roots of those nations affect however not only the history but also patterns of contemporary multiethnic states. Since the nature of the state determines the political decision of its inhabitants, the early state formation sets conditions for those who differ in culture and ethnicity from the dominant or "root nation." This basic rudimentary distinction divides the inhabitants into "in-" and "out-groups," into those who belong to the ruling political community, the early, dominant nation, and "outsiders," descendants of the conquered tribes or later arrivals. Survival of those early perceptions and identities are still with us today.

Some of the basic principles of social organization are "natural." They are simply a consequence of elementary needs and corresponding goals and interests. To this area belong the two elementary and at the same time early primordial human bonds: kinship and consanguinity, hence common descent and neighborhood. In early and traditional societies both are usually fused.

By social bond we understand a set of needs and values, and corresponding goals and interests, as well as norms that prompt association into coherent groups. Here belong common descent groups such as extended families, associated by elementary needs, shared interests and goals, and integrated also by common ancestry or belief in common origin as well as religion. By means of cooperation and mutual aid these coherent groups meet the basic needs of their members and protect them also against hostile out-groups.

The second bond is neighborhood, the fact of territorial proximity. This is also a "natural" association. People living in close vicinity, related by culture, some sentiments or interests, are impelled since early times to associate again in order to meet their basic needs or to defend themselves against hostile out-groups that attempt to invade their territory.

At early stages the very elementary needs impose some of the primordial forms of association. Both bonds—but primarily consanguinity or common descent—combined with memories or beliefs of early or initial occupation of a territory, are at the root of the principles of legitimacy of political power, hence of the right to exercise exclusive control over the territory that the group claims.

Even at the early stages of mankind, as well as among traditional societies, we may trace some forms of political control. It appears as an exclusive exercise of authority over a definite territory. The "positive" aspects of exclusion of the "others" is inclusion of "us"—that is, members of the group or band and in later stages members of the tribe and eventually of the state. Hence it is an elementary form of exercise of authority over a more or less definite piece of land, later called sovereignty.

Very early on, man learned to share the use of certain areas with others, with different peoples. To this early group belong nomadic tribes or bands, food gatherers or hunters, later also pastoral peoples. This sharing of territories, not uncommon among traditional societies, has survived today.

Aristotle, and I suppose other ancient Greek philosophers, made a distinction between social institutions that have their roots in the very nature of man (e.g., *Physis*) and those enacted by his decision as citizen.

Common descent and neighborhood are in a way natural and can be called that. Both are at the very root of the formation of the state. In the early polity, these bonds were fused: common descent, neighborhood, hence territorial, solidarity and religion, a common belief system. The most powerful was probably the common descent bond fused with and reinforced by religion. There was a time span of transition from those early forms of political authority, still in a nascent form, to the advanced form of a state. When the state begins is of course a matter of definition.

The state is identified with a mature political organization, with a firmly established political system, a distinct political authority, a government of some sort, exercising control over a territory. The state already has a differentiated social structure, specialized crafts and functions, an emerging warrior class. Separation of the political authority from the religious one may appear early in some rare cases. Usually, at this stage, political and religious authority are fused.

In what kind of social process was the state formed? There are many theories. Among those theories the dominant one, well advanced in the past century, and even earlier, was the theory of conquest. It is a convincing theory, since some historians have witnessed and recorded this kind of early formation of states.

The theory of conquest can be traced back to the fourteenth-century Arab historian Ibn Khaldoun. Khaldoun was not distant in time from this type of state formation in Arab North Africa. The theory reappears again in French historical writings of the eighteenth century. The conquest theory was however fully developed by Ludwik Guwplowicz, and later by Franz Oppenheimer, at the turn of the nineteenth century and early years of the twentieth. It has been also widely accepted by many scholars.

We have recorded evidence of that recurrent pattern in European history of the middle and latter part of the first millennium, during the Fall of Rome and great invasions from the East. At this time, many of the present nation-states were established. It was a process of conquest by the invading, barbarian tribes, followed by consolidation of power. The conquerors and conquered were different nations, different in language, culture, even attire, often also physically different.

We may introduce a "coercive bond" next to those rooted in common descent or neighborhood. A complex social organization may be formed that way. Force and coercion have been applied widely as a coercive bond of masters and subjects. In its extreme form of total subjugation the weaker was tied to the victor by means of serfdom or by the most oppressive and painful form of subordination—slavery.

New states were established by way of domination and control of physical, military power, while the conquered nationalities were more often than not reduced to a lower-class nationalities status. Later, however, in many cases, cultural assimilation, intermarriage and social adjustment blurred early ethnic-cultural distinctions. In some cases sacred scriptures were quoted to calm religious sentiments and rationalize discrimination.

In Europe's history, however, the conquering tribes assimilated the advanced Roman culture. New nations were formed in the process of fusion of the native, tribal and Roman culture, while most ethnic groups were sooner or later united by a shared, universal religion: Christianity. Still, coercion and naked power was the sole source of authority at the time of subjugation.

As a rule, a lower status was assigned to the conquered nationalities. Later both subjugation and the lower status were rationalized. The disenfranchised minorities—argued the masters—were intellectually, racially or culturally inferior. Legitimacy and dominant rule were reinforced by customs and belief systems, by religion, as well as religious rituals. Coronation, not only a political but also a religious act, became a symbol of legitimacy. Tradition and customs shared by the conquerors and the conquered have grown with time and affected the attitudes and the entire political system.

In ancient history, this was one frequent and perhaps typical way of building a multiethnic state. It was also "natural" in terms of contemporary culture and shared beliefs. In later times slavery and later serfdom were considered a consequence of a natural, even divine order.

In some historical cases, the entire conquered nation as subjugated ethnic groups, was forced into servitude. Usually, various grades and levels of submission and servitude were enforced and sanctioned by rules and laws as well as customs. Hence, the original, multiethnic state that developed this way from an earlier time was divided and structured into ethnoclasses of various levels. When such a state embraced not one but several diverse nationalities, some were often better treated, while others submitted to a harsher, more oppressive rule.

This kind of "differential" discrimination was a kind of social "technique" for governing a vast multiethnic state. Some ethnic groups that were less discriminated against were content with their less oppressive status and did not oppose the rulers. Some, with their special skills and abilities, were helpful in general administration. With time, political attitudes changed while the nature of the regime was often changing as well.

Turkey, the Ottoman Empire, may serve here as an example. Many of the conquered nationalities, whether Serbs or Albanians, converted to Islam; some assisted the Turks and their rule, while a vast majority of Serbs, faithful to the Greek Orthodox Church, opposed Turkish rule.

The Ottoman Empire was divided primarily along religious lines. Islam was the dominant religion and Muslims the ruling class. Conversion to Islam was a way to privileged status. The change of religion and identity was generally considered a betrayal by those who suffered discrimination and refused to abandon their tradition and their ethnic heritage.

The Ottoman Empire has been considered, and still is by many historians, a relatively tolerant state. This is in some way at least historically valid when we compare Turkey of Suleiman with Spain of the Inquisition. In modern Turkish history, however, some nationalities were treated better than others. The Ottoman Empire was indeed relatively tolerant toward Jewish refugees from Spain, who found there a haven and continued to enjoy a tolerant status as well as in the Balkans, for example, the port city of Salonica.

However, Armenians were subject to repetitive persecutions, some ending in very cruel major massacres. The Ottomans were military people; they needed educated Greeks for business and to administrate. Some of this was for mutual benefit though. Greeks suffered many massacres in the nineteenth century at the hands of the Turks. The term *holocaust* has been reintroduced by the Greeks to denote Turkish massacres of Greeks during the nineteenth century: it means to burn everyone alive. And still, Greeks played a prominent role in the economy of the Ottoman Empire, as well as at times in administrative capacities.

The life of a Bulgarian peasant, exploited by Turkish tax collectors was harsh and difficult, but again his religion—to a certain degree—was tolerated. The system worked in strange ways and gave some stability to vast areas inhabited by a variety of nationalities and different religious communities.

Multiethnic states that were built on conquest represent one, even perhaps a dominant, pattern of building of multiethnic states. Various ethnic groups that were subdued were tied to the dominant nation by means of a coercive bond. Once a state was established and reinforced by a system of institutions, given permanence by ways of laws and customs, traditions and beliefs, a historical road was chosen. The future for many years, even centuries to come was decided and usually glorified by historians.

III

But conquest and the coercive bond highlighted just one way of building multiethnic states. Other historical roads also appeared.

The Eastern Mediterranean city-states originated with the growth of population and merger of neighboring communities. It was a process of slow association of the expanding neighboring villages. An early Greek historian and philosopher tells us that Athens was born that way. To use Aristotle's definition: it was also a "natural" process, later formalized by a system of laws and institutions.

Some city-states came into existence by territorial expansion, by growth and meeting neighboring communities. Those city-states grew and were widened within a friendly or cooperative vicinity, by means of a neighborhood bond.

The early beginnings, however, are more often than not buried deep in the past, unrecorded and open to our present conjecture. But even when those early beginnings remain unknown, their impact on our destiny continues.

The maritime trade and port cities may have also played a particular role in the formation of multiethnic urban settlements as was the case of Athens.

Inhabitants of port cities, even in those earlier times were well familiar with foreigners who came to trade and to exchange goods from distant lands and islands (keep in mind, "distant" in light of the time). These foreigners spoke different languages—dialects differed greatly—and wore unusual attire, but brought desired goods. The very fact that trade took place and personal contact was made, however, was not sufficient to induce a broader, even sympathetic attitude toward a stranger.

A friendly approach to a stranger, even a "neutral" one called for a broader world outlook, enriched by curiosity, interest and even appreciation of these differences. The Greeks may have considered outsiders as barbarians, yes, inferiors. On the other hand, however, many Greek writers had a creative curiosity and a friendly interest in those cultural differences. We can notice in the writings of Herodotus, an early Greek historian (more like the father of history), an appreciation, curiosity and intellectual interest when he wrote about the peculiarities of Egyptian or Persian ways of life. This attitude was also a reflection of a broader, general Hellenic outlook.

It seems that a stranger who came to Athens and perhaps to other port cities or trading places, was not necessarily greeted with fear and mistrust or feelings of superiority. Those foreign sailors and traders must have been welcomed in Greek marketplaces since trade was vital for the prosperity, even the very existence, of a commercial port city. Some stayed longer or settled there with a special status; some were even "adopted" according to the customs and laws of the city community.

This was the case in Athens. Major changes took place in Attica about the sixth century B.C. which, after political struggles the ancient organization rooted in principles of common descent has been transformed into a territorial one, based on vicinity and not solely on common descent. Hence, the once consanguinal, tribal, political organization was substantially changed and displaced by a territorial one and by territorial administrative division into *deme*.

Citizenship was extended to all inhabitants of the territorial units of the *deme*, as well as to foreigners. This was a temporary measure, a political move to counterbalance the influence of powerful families. Still, this shift from collective-consanguinal or kinship principle to individual-territorial was of historical significance. It was a major socio-political transformation.

Thus, the political identity of an individual shifted from the tribe, or common descent, to citizenship, to the state. What happened was a process of separation: the separation of ethnicity and the principle of common descent from political membership and identity. A new type of state originated. An individual was now directly associated with the state. The state, Aristotle wrote, was an association of citizens. It was not an association of tribes or clans, using his definition, but an association of individuals. It was not solely an association of people of common descent; even foreigners, as neighbors, could become citizens.

Unlike a multiethnic state created by way of conquest and coercion, here was a multiethnic state that included people of foreign ethnicity. All free inhabitants were included, irrespective of their origin. Citizens were equal before the law, subject to the rules of the same principles. Athenian polity at this time was already a democracy, which implied consensus of those who had a part in government and shared responsibilities and duties. Athens during those few years was a multiethnic city-state, a civic state, an association of citizens, irrespective of their origin.

The role of citizenship as a key political concept was also the beginning of a historical shift from collective to individual. Athens was now an association of individuals, dwelling in neighboring administrative units—*deme*—not an association of collectives of clans and tribes. Tribes continued to exist in a reformed way, now tied to territorial divisions. Responsibility also shifted from collectives to individuals. (We shall return to this theme in chapter 2.)

Athenian reforms were however limited in space and time. Citizenship continued to be exclusive, especially when compared to Rome, where, centuries later, citizenship had been given to members of many allied and conquered tribes and nations. As a rule, an Athenian citizen still had to be born of Athenian parents. Nonetheless, the basic territorial principle had been in a sense "invented," although it had not yet become a major institution of a multiethnic, multinational state or a major principle of nationality policy.

It was Rome—at first the Roman Republic and later the Roman Empire—that reinvented and adopted citizenship as a major policy and an instrument in the construction of a multiethnic state on a universal scale.

The Romans formulated a new model of a multiethnic state, different from those states built by conquest and held together by total subordination of conquered peoples by means of a coercive bond. It was indeed an "invention" or a "discovery" of what we could call until recently a new nationality policy. Today we call it a new ethnic policy, but it was also a new technique for building a multiethnic state.

Athenians and other city-states dwellers were probably the originators of citizenship, of direct association of individuals with the state, which in turn was governed by laws, with the participation of citizens. Hence, they probably borrowed, invented, or discovered this basic civic principle.

The Roman Republic created a variety of different categories of citizenship and extended the civic principle to many conquered or allied peoples. Roman citizenship secured individual rights, even privileges. With time, Roman citizenship became a highly desirable institution, especially attractive to those who were conquered. In many cases Romans did not differ in their war-making. They were ruthless and cruel in their conquests. But, in some cases they offered citizenship to the defeated and hence an equal status with the victors. Compare this nationality policy to the policy of Nazi Germany or to German minor satellites.

Roman citizenship was inclusive rather than exclusive, as was Greek citizenship. True—the Roman Republic, although it introduced this principle, was not yet as generous as the later Roman Empire. It was no longer the principle of common descent and ethnic kinship, but rather the territorial principle of a common bond, a civic principle of membership in the same state, that integrated the empire.

Citizenship was quite different from "subjectship." A citizen was a free person protected by courts and laws. The subject of an oriental autocrat was not sheltered by the rule of law and individual rights. In times of the empire, Rome embraced vast territories in Europe, North Africa, and Asia. It was a truly multiethnic state. All those diverse nationalities, speaking different languages and worshipping different gods, were united by and shared a common identity—a Roman identity—thanks to a common Roman citizenship.

The Roman Empire was not a "benign, humane" polity. Cruelty in their games and the ruthlessness of their emperors affected the culture. But at the same time, the rule of law and legal order continued, as did relative freedom of expression. Moreover, some of the republican institutions survived and continued. But again, it was a slave society. The social system and the economy was built on this oppressive foundation.

The Roman Empire inherited many republican institutions, among them citizenship, and by the third century A.D., citizenship has been extended to all free inhabitants of the empire, notwithstanding religion or origin. Ethnicity has been separated from the state; all subjects were granted the same rights.

Citizenship was a major Roman institution and also an unusual legal and political device for building a multiethnic state. It was a political bond between the state and an individual. Citizenship was a historical fruit of the Greeks and Romans, of the city-states. Great multiethnic empires of Asia or Egypt were built in a different manner.

Greek city-states and initially the Roman Republic did not create large empires, like those of Asia. Greeks and later Romans were "urban" peoples. Their typical polities were city-states governed by assemblies under rule of law.

Greek city-states expanded by way of colonies, new city-states. Another way of constructing new states was to establish one: Rome was established that way according to ancient legends (*urbs condita*—a founded city). Democracy was limited only to small, urban political communities, and not all city-states were necessarily democratic. Colonies were centers of trade and industry. Unlike the great Asian empires, the Greeks did not annex large territories. Democracy, which involved participation of citizens in government, in enacting laws, was not practiced by other large ancient empires. It was difficult indeed to apply a democratic system, for example, the Athenian form of government over a wide and multiethnic territory.

Alexander of Macedon changed this policy and extended his empire over three continents and adopted an oriental autocratic model of state building. Alexander's empire was, however, humanized thanks to Greek philosophy and tradition. Nonetheless, Alexander was deified and also became a supreme sovereign.

Similarly Rome, while expanding far beyond its neighboring territory, changed the form of an ancient republic into an empire with a deified ruler. The state was "orientalized," but Roman law as well as some basic republican institutions (e.g., citizenship) continued and extended now to many foreign nations.

Roman citizenship was a historical milestone, particularly as a technique in building a multiethnic state. Moreover, it marked a shift from collective responsibility or servitude of a conquered nation to recognizing the individual rights of a person. A kinship or common descent bond, in the construction of a state was displaced by citizenship, by a political bond between an individual and the state. The institution of citizenship also marks the beginning of a necessary balance between an individual and the state as the "collective."

IV

After the Fall of Rome the institution of citizenship did not share the fate of the empire. It did not disappear. Citizenship continued in Italian cities and, with urban development, it slowly spread all over continental Europe. Citizenship survived in European cities enriched by native institutions, laws and cultures.

The civic institution carried the creed of liberty and rights of a person. With time, the concept of individual human, civil and political rights became a part of European political and legal culture and spread widely from its original sources.

In medieval times, citizenship however was only an urban institution; it did not embrace the entire nation. The clergy and nobility enjoyed a privileged status, as did the cities, although to a lesser extent. The peasantry in most of countries were reduced to serfdom. But the movement toward extension of basic rights and freedoms appeared rather early, especially in England.

Cities also had immigrants or mixed populations of different ethnic origin, of different denominations, speaking different languages. Not unlike ancient Romans, they too acquired citizenship.

Citizenship became closely connected with the growth of rationalism and eighteenth-century Enlightenment. The philosophy of natural law and social contract that has affected Western political thought was articulated in the very concept of an association of free men, of a political system based on consensus and contract of its members.

The fundamental theory of social contract was simple: the state in its beginning was the fruit of an agreement of free men. Free men, by means of a voluntary contract, a social contract, established the state and delegated political authority. The theory was false but convincing and at the same time constructive. It was this false theory that made a contribution to the rise of a more humane and benevolent state and democratic institution.

The United States were from the start a political association that elevated the Bill of Rights to a supreme law. Slavery, however, extended the struggle for full extension of these principles until far into the nineteenth century, although some of the member states abolished slavery earlier in the eighteenth century.

U.S. citizens were of diverse ethnic origin from the very beginnings of their republic. Most were of British descent, but many were German, some were of French, Dutch, Polish, Jewish and other ancestry. They differed also in religion, but all were U.S. citizens. In this sense, citizenship was an all-inclusive, multiethnic institution. It was a broader denomination than ethnic alone that united all members of the state, however, there were exceptions. Slaves and the native American population did not share the basic freedoms of others.

It was the French Revolution that elevated citizenship to a key symbol of the republic. The division into estates was abolished and citizenship in France became all-inclusive; all "good patriots" were considered Frenchmen. France and the French Revolution created the political folklore and symbolism of citizenship. It was both a legal and symbolic expression of a new republican order. Hence, citizenship marked a historical shift, indeed a revolutionary one, from the medieval system of corporations and estates—in a word "collectives"—to the individual, to the person.

Inspiration favoring a democratic form of government came from antiquity but above all from the example of the English people, who for centuries moved toward a free and more democratic political order, creating a well-working, though at times turbulent Parliament and an efficient parliamentary government.

Ancient Greece and Rome as well as English experience and influence were not the only sources of inspiration or political models. Political philosophers in France, England, Italy and other European countries suggested in their books new and inspiring theories for a better society and state, that owed its strength to the will and consent of citizens. Books and newspapers were now available and new creeds were diffused widely; the fifteenth-century invention of the printing press made its decisive impact three centuries later. Historical time and social ideas moved more slowly than in our times, but far more rapidly than in the times of the Greeks and Romans.

In the United States, at the very beginning of the Union, citizenship was an expression of a voluntary association of free men, who enjoyed equal rights under the rule of law. The country was however divided into free men and slaves. Even after Emancipation, discrimination of the African, Native Indian and Oriental minorities continued *de jure* and *de facto*.

It took almost a century before discrimination in public policies ended. By the middle of the twentieth century, the United States became an advanced model of a civic, pluralistic and multiethnic state, a democratic polity inhabited by a variety of native and immigrant ethnic and racial groups, sometimes greatly differing in cultures, customs and of course language. Citizenship once again became a major institution in the constitution of a multiethnic political community. Not since the Roman times was a multiethnic civic state instituted with such clarity and constancy of purpose.

V

The United States is not the only civic state of course; other democracies especially immigrant states instituted similar policies. Laws and policies differ since nations differ in political culture and tradition. The basic principles of those multiethnic states are however similar. Today what makes the U.S. experiment unique and comparable to Rome is the unusual variety of ethnic groups and relative success in unifying the country by means of a civic principle. As it was centuries ago in Rome, the presence of large and diverse minorities is not a source of weakness but, to the contrary, an element of strength and worldwide influence. (More extensive discussion of this follows in chapter 4.)

The essence of a civic state lies in a common denominator, that is, a common identity shared by all diverse ethnic or cultural groups. This common denominator is citizenship. Its meaning has a more universal quality than ethnicity, race or religion. Citizenship is an articulation of an inclusive political association and common culture that unites all inhabitants of diverse ethnicity, religion or race. The Romans "invented" this common denominator and made it a major institution in building a multiethnic empire. The United States applied the full meaning of citizenship in building a democratic and pluralistic, multiethnic republic.

The civic state is unified by means of a territorial, political bond and customs and not merely by one of common, ethnic origin, as tribal, particularly nationalistic, states are. All inhabitants, irrespective of race, religion, ethnicity or cultural difference are members of a political community—the state. They are citizens, and the state is an association of citizens, all free; and all have the same rights and carry respective duties.

The United States is not only a tolerant country, a country that recognizes differences. It is also a pluralistic nation, composed of members of a variety of ethnic groups, who at the same time are Americans, members of a political community and who enjoy the same political and civil human rights. This dual identity, ethnic and political, is neither denied nor incompatible. Historical civic states mark a decisive shift from a common descent bond to the political, territorial and cultural bond in the development of a multiethnic state.

The civic bond is also a consequence of the separation of the ethnic bond from the political, in a similar (but not identical) way that religion has been separated from the state. This fundamental departure from the early, as well as from a contemporary, tribal state implies a fusion of religion, ethnicity and political identity.

VI

The history of two major kinds of multiethnic states—the tribal nationalistic and tolerant civic—is part of the very history of democracy and political rights. This history is not solely of academic interest.

Nationalistic states, in their extreme form, built on common descent bond and the idea of a single, exclusive identity, on the lore of common origin, which resulted in political systems of discrimination of minorities, policies of expulsion and deportation, and in extreme cases, tribalism that led to massacres of weaker ethnic communities, extermination, and eventually to genocide, holocaust and the "ethnic cleansing" of our times.

Contrariwise the civic state, rooted in neighborhood, territorial solidarity and common culture secured equal rights for all inhabitants and paved the road toward a more benign, humane polity, benign to all. The civic principle reconciled two identities: the ethnic, of common ethnic culture, and broader civic, an identity based on belonging to the same state and also sharing a broader, national culture and institutions of the common nation-state.

The model of a nationalistic tribal state resulted in a polity of discrimination of diverse ethnic groups. It is adverse to any form of a widely tolerant, humane, democratic polity. Civic principle and citizenship offer a variety of patterns of benevolent multiethnic states and suggest viable alternatives in construction of the latter.

The government of a civic or tolerant state does not control or interfere with the activities of a variety of ethnic, religious or cultural groups who do enjoy freedom of association. Freedom of speech secures freedom of any cultural expression.

Ethnic identification in a civic state does not result in any civic impediment or deprivation of access to opportunities. In tribal, nationalistic states opportunities are open solely to those who can claim that their ancestry belonged to the dominant nationality, to the historical "core" nation. The policy of equal opportunity was and is enforced by means of affirmative action, at times even to the disadvantage of members of the majority, members of the root nation, or, even paradoxically, contrary to the principles of equal opportunity for all. (The evaluation of these policies is not a matter that shall be considered in this volume.)

The modern democratic and civic state is not an ideal state or a perfect one. Furthermore, our approach is concerned primarily with the ethnic and political aspects of the state, not with its social or economic problems. But it is a benevolent polity, it does exist and it works well. It has worked—we may add—thus far. Its success and workability depends, as always, not only on the nature of institutions, but also on the quality of citizens and those who govern. In the end, it is the quality of men and women that determines the smooth working and efficiency of the government.

It is a kind of political system that cannot be imposed easily by force on an opposing nation with a different political culture or on active, political majorities. However, a variety of tolerant measures and benevolent systems can be instituted with outside support and international pressure. This had been done in some major European states after the Second World War.

Change in public policies toward minorities is a basic issue that causes problems and calls for an extensive discussion. Nevertheless, during the important historical period of the last fifty years we have learned that nations should be considered as members of a wider community, a community of nations.

In such a context, people may expect aid and assistance when in need, but only if they respect a shared set of rules and elementary norms. On the other hand, as members of such a wider community, they must also share responsibilities. Within such a community, pressures and decisions made by international authorities backed by force and even sanctions have an impact. It is true that attitudes cannot be changed easily. But international pressures, sometimes diplomatic intervention, even the pressure of worldwide public opinion, especially with today's mass media, do affect general public policies, particularly policies toward minorities. At least some protection had been given in the past by international authorities through intervention.

In many cases some kind of order was restored and discriminatory and oppressive public policies were mitigated at least in a few visible instances. In some cases international sanctions and public opinion affect national public policies, and public policies on the other hand, in a long process may affect attitudes by way of education. We have witnessed at least the beginning of such changes in Bosnia and Herzegovina in Europe and Rwanda in Africa. We shall limit our discussion here to this short comment.

The traditional and historical definition of citizenship has been broadened in our times. Responsibilities of the state have been extended to social areas, including social welfare. Included in this wide social sphere are labor rights and legislation, old age and health insurance and assistance during times of unemployment—these areas being only a small part of the complex system of a virtual labor code of our times. Social legislation reinforces even more the political bond of a multiethnic state (more about this in Chapter 4).

In spite of the extension of the nature and definition of a modern citizenship (or perhaps thanks to this broad definition), a civic state suggests a workable model for a multiethnic society. A civic organization can be applied however by states that practice a variety of different social-economic systems—for example, those that practice a wide, free market system and others that follow a model of a mixed economy, as well as those with wide areas of state intervention.

Thus far the U.S. experiment has been quite successful in building a civic multiethnic state. However signs of opposing forces have appeared, such as groups and individuals opposed to any type of a tolerant multiethnic society, especially to those of different races or religions. These groups are vocal and active.

The political fate of a nation is not always decided by its majorities. Small, armed groups may terrorize a nation by means of ruthless and brutal violence. Political terror of the few may generate fear in millions.

Public policies that are free of discrimination are not tantamount to the absence of prejudice. The government by means of education, public policies and court decisions may influence social attitudes and shared norms and values. But attitudes and sentiments do not change easily.

A civic system calls, however, for vigorous support by a critical section of a nation. By critical, we mean large groups of voters, influential enough, tolerant and educated, sufficient in number and influence to make this difficult but humane political system an efficient and workable one.

There is also a limit as to how many peoples of a widely different culture a nation can absorb. Today, some states may have already reached a kind of "saturation" point. The level of cultural difference of both majority and minority are also relevant. Some nations, due to tradition, culture and education, accept far more easily a neighborhood of distinct ethnic newcomers, while others are not only adverse but are hostile toward the display of any minor cultural differences.

VII

Economic change on a historical scale and globalization of our economy tied to technological change has already affected our society. Cities once inhabited by a single historical nationality, with few "outsiders" of different language or culture, became multiethnic. Ethnic diversity also affected old, historical nation-states. It is a social reality that cannot be reversed.

Our future, even survival, depends more and more on our abilities and skills to live in a neighborhood with "others" who differ in culture, religion or language, and we have to learn to share responsibilities in spite of our differences. Nations today are far more interdependent, and our existence and well-being depends far more on the work and prosperity of others, neighbors as well as far more distant people, than ever in the past. In consequence, effective building of well-working multiethnic communities and states and proper ethnic policies are issues of major significance.

Citizenship, tied to the state and broader culture but not necessarily to common descent, a "common denominator" shared by all inhabitants, has been an effective institution, an effective instrument applied to the construction of a multiethnic state. It is an ancient institution that continues through two and a half millennia of our history. Weakening its essential meaning and function may affect not only the state, but also our entire culture.

A comprehensive survey of how this long historical citizenship road was shaped and matured contributes to our understanding of the nature of this major institution. Thus, we shall begin the next chapter with Greece and Rome and end with the United States of today. In the very philosophy of constructing a multiethnic state there is a challenging similarity between Rome and the American Republic.[1] There are, of course, basic differences regarding the very nature of the state and social order.

NOTE

1. On the origin and definition of state see Feliks Gross, *The Civic and the Tribal State: The State, Ethnicity, and the Multiethnic State* (Westport, Conn.: Greenwood Press, 1998), chapter 1. This book is a continuation of a major theme: the multiethnic state.

2

THE ROOTS OF CITIZENSHIP: ATHENS AND ROME

Never any state was . . . so open to receive strangers into their body as were the Romans; therefore, it sorted with them accordingly, for they grew to the greatest monarchy. Their manner was to grant naturalization (which they called "jus civitatis" [right of citizenship]), and to grant it in the highest degree, that is not only "jus comercii" [right of trading], "jus connubii" [right of intermarriage], "jus haereditatis" [right of inheritance]; but, also, "jus sufragii" [right of suffrage], and "jus honorum" [right of honors]; and this not to singular persons alone, but likewise to whole families; yea, to cities and sometimes to nations. Add to this their custom of plantation of colonies, whereby the Roman plant was removed into the soil of other nations, and, putting both constitutions together, you will say, that it was not the Romans that spread upon the world, but it was the world that spread upon the Romans; and that was the sure way of greatness.

Francis Bacon, "On Greatness of Kingdoms and
Estates" (1612, 1625), *Essays and Wisdom of the Ancients*,
Preface by B. Montague (New York: Nelson Little Brown Co., 1884).

ATHENS

Where are the beginnings? How did it start? The fundamental principles of our society are ancient indeed. The roots of many institutions, customs and laws, even daily habits, originated centuries ago. Once established, they have a tendency to continue as long as they function, adjusting at times to changes or affecting the very changes. Some disappear, others continue sometimes against the logic of times, by the very strength of habituation and custom. Hence the full meaning, their rationality or irrationality can be better understood in a historical outlook and context, in viewing first its historical advance and changes and, second, relating an institution or custom to the historical situation within which it appeared, so that we can see how it works within a different polity and society of distant historical times. The lines written by Henry Sumner Maine in 1861 have not lost their validity: "If by any means we can determine the early forms of jural conceptions, they will be invaluable to us. These rudimentary ideas are to jurist what the primary crusts of earth are to the geologist. They contain, potentially, all the forms which law has subsequently exhibited itself."[1] Nothing in our culture, nor a single case in politics can be understood without history; ahistorism is tantamount to cultural and political illiteracy.

Since the nature of the civic state is directly tied to and reflected in the development of citizenship, understanding of this institution and the way it has developed is seminal to our case. Thus, we shall try to trace the genealogy of modern citizenship and to follow the long development of this institution in an attempt to discover how it happened and how the civic state came into being.

The early beginnings of citizenship appear in ancient Greece, in the ancient Greek city-states. Citizenship in its early history is closely related to what was, at that time, a democratic government, democratic in the sense of participation of members of a state in public business and in government. The fundamental significance of this institution in Greek culture is reflected in those extensive discussions of philosophers and statesmen on citizenship. Aristotle writes: "The citizen in strict sense is best defined by one criterion, a man who shares in the administration of justice and in the holding of office."[2] In an introductory chapter to his *Politics*, Aristotle writes about the early lawgiver Solon: "Solon himself would seem to have given the people only the necessary minimum of power. He gave them simply the right of electing the magistrates and calling them to account, and if the people do not enjoy these elementary rights, they must be a people of slaves, and the enemies of government."[3] Thus, in its early beginnings, Athenian citizenship was associated with a democratic state, democratic in terms of government by consent and decision. In his final definition Aristotle argues: "He who enjoys the right of sharing in deliberative judicial office (for any period of fixed or unfixed time) attains thereby the status of a citizen of his state and a state, in its simplest terms, is a body of such persons, adequate in number for achieving a self-sufficient existence." The Athenian citizenship—continues the philosopher from Stagira—is not unique. There are other forms of citizenship, but different in their meaning, such as in Carthage and Sparta.

What is relevant here is that Aristotle points to a different social-political bond, different than the traditional, we may even say "natural" one, hence consanguinity and kinship—we may call it today "ethnicity" in its early form of tribal solidarity. Citizenship here is a distinct political bond—the relationship of an individual to other citizens organized in a state and to the city-state as a political territorial community, distinct from kinship or consanguinity, distinct from the tribe. This relation to the state is articulated in participation of its members in the conduct of public life. In its early form, citizenship is not yet separated from kinship—that happened later—nonetheless a citizen is defined by his public, political function. But, the city is inhabited by a variety of people. How can one become a citizen? "For practical reason," writes Aristotle, "one usually defines a citizen as one born of citizen parents," moreover this has to be traced three, even four generations back. He quotes Gorgias: "As mortars are made by the craftsmen, so Laurissans are persons who are made by the 'craftsmen who are Laurissan makers.' "[4] True, citizenship is defined now by birth and is not related to a tribe anymore but to the city-state. In consequence, by the fourth century B.C. citizenship in Athens was traced to parents, but defined by Aristotle not only by birth but also in terms of its political function. Even the origin is tied to the concept of state as a political-territorial community and not to a tribe, not to what is today called "ethnicity." Hence, the definition of an Athenian citizen rested on state, territory and culture and not solely on birth. "To be a fellow citizen," continues Aristotle, "is to be sharers in one state, and to have one state is also to have one place of residence."[5] Culture, or what we today call culture, appears early as a test of Hellenic identity. Isocrates argues that Greeks are those who have Greek culture (education—*paideia*), and a historian takes pride that the founder of mathematics, Thales, was born in Miletos, while his mother was Phoenician.

To be a Greek Athenian citizen was a privilege. The Greek orator Demosthenes pointed out that "the Athenian people regarded their citizenship to be something so worthy and august that they passed laws strictly prescribing its bestowal."[6] Nonetheless citizenship was rather a privilege; it was a privilege of a fraction of the entire population.

From its recorded beginning Athens had a diverse population, people of dissimilar origins and views. We learn from Thucydides that political exiles from various Greek cities sought refuge in this port city. There were, of course, also many foreign traders and merchants who were not citizens. And we should not forget that with all its democratic institutions Athens was a slave society. Foreigners were distinguished by their distinct status; *Metoikoi* were foreigners of special status; they had a legal identity, had some rights but also had military duties and paid taxes. Metoikoi were not citizens, hence did not partake in government. *Proxenoi* in turn were foreigners living in a foreign city but were representing and taking care of the interests of Athens. They were rewarded with special privileges, including legal safeguards. They shared some honors and were invited to communal feasts.[7] Furthermore *Xenoi* were temporary guests, foreigners who visited Athens. Some of them probably settled after a time, not unlike those who arrive today to the great port city of New York on tourist visas. But above all, the most numerous were *douloi*—slaves. Women and children were not included but enjoyed legal rights and protection through their citizen husbands and fathers.

As early as the fourth century B.C. a practice of exchanging citizenship—*isopoliteia*—broadened the bond, in a way, with the citizens of other associated cities.[8] It was a civic identity, a civic bond and not a tribal one, that was extended to members of a foreign city-state.

Greece at that time had a flourishing culture and extensive commerce. Greek merchants and scholars travelled widely, traded and lectured, exchanged ideas and experience, and at times moved and settled in other city-states.

Citizens, however, did not form a majority of inhabitants. Their numbers changed, of course, during Athens' long history, but using a rough estimate the active citizen class, male from 16 to 66 years of age was no larger than perhaps 18 percent of the entire population.

Estimates of ancient statistics are tentative and difficult to ascertain. The demography of Athens was the subject of numerous and extensive studies. Most scholars estimate the number of citizens during the fourth and fifth centuries from about 30,000 or 40,000 to about 60,000 persons. Hauser, for example, indicates that to run the extensive democratic Athenian institutions in the age of Demosthenes, no less than 30,000 adult men were needed.[9] The number of those in military service (*hoplites* and landless *thetes*) amounted to about 43,000. The male population in the age group of 18 to 60 at this time was estimated at 25 percent of the total (wives, children and those over 60), hence Gomme's estimates for total citizen family population was about 172,000. In addition, there were about 28,500 *metiks* (metoikoi) and 115,000 slaves; the total population of Attica in the fifth and fourth centuries B.C. amounted perhaps to about 315,000. The estimates vary of course. Jones estimates 124,000 as total free persons (free Athenian male adults, female and children).[10]

Athens was an active, "participatory" democracy. Its assembly (*ekklesia*) was attended by no less than 6,000 citizens, and thousands were appointed by lot.[11] Politics absorbed a substantial amount of time, week by week, month by month. This called for a class with ample leisure and free time who were willing to devote the time to politics and public affairs rather than to more simple pleasures. A large slave population created conditions of leisure for those who were free. It was a democracy of the free within a slave society.

Athens and Athenians should be however considered within a historical context, as compared to Sparta or contemporary Persia. This was not an ideal, free state. Far from it. Citizens were privileged, free, protected by law. Citizens were males—women could not own property or decide about marriage. Nevertheless, through citizenship of their husbands, they enjoyed the protection of law. Athenian citizens, at least for a long time, were not subject—as slaves were—to torture (moreover higher penalties were given for murdering Athenians).[12] Their politics, unlike philosophy, was not necessarily humane and magnanimous. Thucydides tells us that they were hated by their allies and subject people. Presumably in Mytilene more than a thousand rebels were executed.[13] This was not an exceptional or unique case.

Although citizenship during Kleisthenes' time (sixth century B.C.) evolved for a brief time indeed into a political and civic bond, it was still tied to its tribal roots. Kleisthenes' reforms were fundamental but prompted by temporary, political conditions and struggles, they did not transform this institution into a strong civic bond as the Roman reformers would do. Athens remained an endogamic society. Mixed marriages were not condoned. Those of "impure" birth who claimed Athenian citizenship were often sold into slavery. "Ethnic cleansing" or purges (*disephismos*) occurred early in times of the tyranny, but also occurred later even under Pericles. Those of "impure" birth were struck from the register and often sold. In 345 B.C. the law was milder and Athenian status was voted by fellow citizens in the *deme* (community). Those who lost were given the status of *metoikoi*, legalized foreigners. Plutarch tells us that during the glorious days of Pericles 5,000 of the "purged" citizens were sold into slavery.

But let us stress again that this citizenship has to be considered in its historical context. Endogamy was strong in Athens, but it was still more rigid in other cultures. In the biblical lore, shortly after the Hebrews settled in the Promised Land, Phineas, a priest and grandson of Aaron, killed a Jew and his foreign wife because both violated the law that prohibited mixed marriages. Endogamy was strong in many ancient societies and neither the Greeks nor the Jews were an exception. On the other hand, in their own way, Athenians tolerated foreigners and gave them special status as metiks, contemptuous as this word may seem today. They observed the rule of law in a different way than the Hebrews; they had respect for an individual and his differing views (to a limit of course). They practiced, even "invented" a kind of democracy-instituted citizenship.

Citizenship in Athens was a nascent, future universal Western institution, born on a borderline of diverse civilizations. It was not adopted by the powerful neighboring Asiatic autocracies.

The Athenian democratic institutions did not diffuse in the way that Roman citizenship did and evolve into a universal political bond. Nonetheless the Greek experience had a lasting impact on the development of the very concept of human bond and humanity. Their stoic philosophy affected the Hellenistic world. The idea of *kosmopolis*—a Greek stoic concept—broke the walls of ethnic and tribal boundaries. Athenians frowned upon mixed marriages, but Alexander, a Macedonian and a Greek, fostered mixed marriages and "transethnic" political bonds paving the way to the future religious and political universalism.

History is ambivalent, or, if one prefers, moves on many and not a single track.

Transition to Territorial-Political Citizenship

Until the time of Kleisthenes (sixth century B.C.), citizenship in Athens was primarily associated with consanguinity, kinship bond. The revolutionary change came with the transition from an exclusive kinship bond, the clan and tribal one, to neighborhood, to the political, territorial solidarity and organization. This shift from tribal to territorial, from consanguinity to neighborhood organization and solidarity took place, even if only temporary, in the sixth century B.C. probably as a result of a historical process associated with political changes as well as with a development of a new ideological outlook. This change was not solely in organization of the city-state; it was also a change of principles, a transition from a consanguineal solidarity of common descent, the traditional, in a sense "natural," blood solidarity to the emphasis on territorial proximity, solidarity and neighborhood.

The crucial reforms came after the expulsion of tyrants, when Kleisthenes introduced a new organization based on small, territorial communities, called *deme*, displacing the old, consanguineal bonds of clans and tribes, narrowing their political relevance. Kleisthenes accepted into the deme foreigners, making them a part of the Athenian polity. In *Politics* Aristotle records that he

> distributed Athens into ten tribes, instead of the previous four, with the object of mixing them up so that more might share rights of citizen. From this arose the saying "the prying into tribes as to retort to those wishing to enquire into ancestry ... as he divided the country by demes, into thirty parts, ten in the city area, ten around the coast, ten inland. Those he called tritties and assigned them by lot to each tribe, so that each should share in all three regions."[14]

Thus Kleisthenes introduced a territorial organization weakening the early, traditional, consanguineal and tribal. This, it seems, was his major objective, to weaken the political influence of powerful families. His reforms stress territorial neighborhood identification instead of the traditional blood relationship.

To reinforce the neighborhood solidarity the Athenian reformer also changed the way of naming individuals and families. He changed, or tried to tie the names to the place of origin, (*toponyms*), to change from consanguineal kinship or clan names to territorial neighborhood names, identified by deme, so that new citizens could not be distinguished from the old.[15] A new territorial identity makes its historical entrance in an effort to weaken clan and tribal bonds. Moreover, Kleisthenes' reforms replaced the traditional tribes (*phylai*) with tribes of his own "invention," artificial communities not rooted in blood relation, in kinship. Athenians were still related by clans and brotherhood—we learn from Aristotle's account—and kept their tribal priesthood. At the same time, however, local territorial religious rites were also instituted. Hence, the rites and patrons shifted too, from tribal consanguineal to local territorial deities of the neighborhood. What was emerging, was a new territorial-political *polis*, a wide political community of those who inhabited the same territory and were qualified as citizens. Aristotle writes also about the leaders of popular parties who tried to strengthen the influence of the people by extending citizenship to those who were not born from citizens, who had only one citizen parent or who were illegitimate. "Kleisthenes of Athens," Aristotle continues, "sought to advance the cause of democracy and extended citizenship to a new class, reduced private family cults, introduced in their stead common cults in public centers, to make all the citizens mix, as much as they possibly can to break down their old loyalties."[16]

What was the essence of Kleisthenes' revolution? First, to make a transition from tribal, consanguineal, traditional organization to political organization, anchored in the city-state. Second, transition from tribal, ethnic solidarity, to neighborhood, hence territorial solidarity. In consequence a new kind of citizenship was born, a citizenship associated with the state rather than tribe, a political citizenship. Kleisthenes' reforms were built, however, on old existing institutions that were now used and developed but had their roots in the past. Hence, they were not fully "invented" but rather used to fit the political objectives of the time and gained a new meaning when filled with a new content. Centuries later, this type of citizenship integrated various culturally diverse "ethnics" of the Roman Empire. It was Rome that advanced this political institution and made it a crucial instrument in building a world empire.

Tribal consanguineal solidarity had, however, its relevance. It did not disappear and continued also in religious cults. But this general shift toward a broader, nonconsanguineal concept of citizenship was a historical moment of transition, the early step toward a broader democratic political organization, later toward a distant utopia of a kosmopolis—a universal polity, a world society—but also a simple recognition of the imperatives of neighborhood. A new concept of solidarity had to appear before a broader philosophical concept of humanity and kosmopolis could make its appeal to the sentiments and imagination of the Hellenic philosophers.

Deme

Attica had 139 demes. A deme was a relatively small community similar to a kind of village or neighborhood community. Roughly estimated, a deme had from five hundred to two thousand inhabitants, some were smaller, some larger. Hauser, in his careful statistical estimates, tells us that there were considerable variations in the size of a deme.[17]

Thus deme was a "primary group," a kind of a social unit within which people knew each other, since they were living in the same "place," in a vicinity. Thus their bond was also "natural" since they faced similar problems and had to help each other often in their daily chores and assist in times of emergency simply to survive. They were neighbors and *demotes*. Those men and women, as well as children, irrespective of their origin were in frequent contact with much familiarity. They might have hated each other, at times, but conditions of life impose certain imperatives of solidarity and help, a relationship that a French historian called "relations de bon voisinage"—good neighborhood.[18] This meaning of the term *deme, demiotic*, is often revealed in a semantic association of those terms. Demotes, members of a deme, were also called neighbors (*geitones*) of one another; there is also a "semantic overlap" of *demotes* and *philoi-pheiloi* meaning both friends and kin. Demotes were often philoi indeed.[19] Deme was a community, and the neighborhood bonds between those "face to face" groups were indeed real and strong.

This type of relationship cannot be created by a decree, a decision, a political reform. Roots of those communities were natural, traditional; even while not formalized, they existed early on. We learn that Homer used this term to denote inhabitants of a district.[20] Deme developed from its earlier roots and was strengthened and used by Kleisthenes in order to create a new and strong "infrastructure" of a political system that would counterbalance the tribal organizations controlled and influenced by aristocratic families.[21]

Manville stresses that "the Kleisthenic deme was not invented out of thin air, but were rather newly defined within the social landscape that reflected their evolution."[22] Local demotic religious cults and rites were created and propagated, and cults and rites strengthened the communal bond of the deme. To be a citizen was also expressed in religious terms: to share sacred things.[23]

Religion, religious rites, beliefs and cults are not separate in ancient societies but are part of political and social institutions—they integrate individuals and groups. Patron saints of today continue to identify the communal and individual identity of an Italian village whether in Giulio Veneto in the north or in Campagna. More so in ancient societies, sacred functions and hero worship reinforced the neighborhood solidarity of the demes.

Territorial identification, toponyms, appeared also in names, as we have indicated earlier.[24] This too, probably had some earlier cultural roots, tradition and usage. Now, a demesman from Eleusis was Eleusinos. When patronyms were also used, the toponyms point to a different bond than the clan, tribe or family, and here is its relevance. The toponym was indicative of a new political order, a new loyalty tied to the territorial neighborhood and eventually to the city-state. The use of territorial names points to such a change. Tribal-nomadic peoples could not apply the territorial principle to their names. The difference is striking if one compares biblical names. They are, of course, of different historical times and culture but, nonetheless, point to the nature of social bond. To open the Bible at random (Samuel 19), we read, "This was a man of Benjamin, whose name was Kish, the son of Abiel, the son of Zerior, the son of Bechorath, the son of Aplian, a Benjamite, a mighty man of power." Here, the identification, as well as the social bond (a system of duties and rights) goes by tribe and family. Compare this with Greek names: Aristotle from Stagira, Thales from Miletos, Thukidides the Athenian. Here Greeks are clearly identified not by tribe or family, but by political territory—the city-state. The toponyms, naming by places of origin, probably also had an older tradition in Greece, which was after all in a context of those times an urban society.

Citizenship had been fully formed probably by the year 500 B.C. It was the fruit of statesmanship, of wise decisions by Athenian leaders, with the active support and approval of the people of Attica. Decisions alone could not create such a complex and, in its difference, unusual institution. The development of citizenship was possible within a certain political culture, within a system of values and beliefs shared by large sections of the politically active population. It was a result of a long and unique political process, but once the basic concept was firmly established, the institution became a cultural watershed between the Hellenic, later Western world and the oriental autocracy.

A new political bond, the direct bond of an individual with a state, had been adopted, with a government shared by members of the state, whose legitimacy of power, in addition to religious beliefs, called for the consent of the governed and the rule of law. Furthermore a new identity was stressed, a territorial identity fused with a political identity. Until then it was kinship and religion that tied people together; in great empires of the East, religion combined with naked power.

True, this territorial political identity prevailed in Greece briefly, during the time of Kleisthenes when citizenship was extended almost to all inhabitants of the deme, in a kind of *ius soli*, when persons inhabiting the territory of Attica acquired citizenship, membership in the state, irrespective of their consanguineal ties. This was a revolution indeed. Shortly after this process of integration however, Athenians returned to the principles of *ius sanguinis*, blood and kinship principle, in acquiring citizenship. Nonetheless, a new loyalty had matured and a new legal and working institution thrived.

The territorial nature of citizenship had its distinct ethical and civic content.[25] Manville points to the philosophical nature of citizenship but what seems relevant to me, is that it was also a pragmatic one; it was an idea that "worked." Its essential quality, true, was ethical, normative—to again quote Aristotle, "it provided justice and morally improved citizens." Citizenship was a pragmatic legal institution, yet, but from its early times it cannot be considered as a purely and solely legal institution. Aristotle's comments on citizenship in his *Politics* and *Constitution of Athens* are better understood when compared to his *Ethics*.

Thus, Athenians created a new political institution that protected an individual, opened historical paths toward liberty and humanity to come centuries later. Athenians were probably the first to separate, albeit for a short time, tribal ties and what we today call "ethnicity" from the political structure. It was Kleisthenes who, as Aristotle recorded, would mix up the inhabitants, so that more could share in citizenship.

But Athenian citizenship was not a dynamic universal institution, as it became later in the Roman Empire. It was in a sense a "local" and urban Mediterranean phenomenon limited to a city-state; it was not extended generously by the Athenians to others, as the Romans did. True, it was associated with a democracy but a capricious one. The town meetings of Attica, called *ekklesia*, could banish or expel a citizen by a majority vote. In a sense, it was still a discriminatory institution, limited to a fraction of inhabitants. It was even divisive.[26] Moreover, Athens was a slave society, and slavery in mines and public works was brutal and cruel.[27] With all those considerations, Athenians created an initial form of one of the fundamental institutions of personal freedom and rational government: citizenship in a democracy under a rule of law.

ROME

Roman Citizenship

We have traced the beginning of modern citizenship to ancient Hellas, particularly to Athens. In Greece, foreigners were only exceptionally accepted with full rights into the political community. Still, with the exception of Kleisthenes' reforms, Athenians were as a rule of Athenian ancestry as mixed marriages were not tolerated, save in exceptional cases. There were however some beginnings of a more universal concept of citizenship. Honorary citizenship was granted to some Greeks. After the fourth century B.C. citizenship exchange (*isopoliteia*) was developed, which was also extended to entire communities, granting basic rights of commerce, *connubium*, marriage and right to own land.[28] Here we can trace the beginnings, perhaps an initial stage of extension of citizenship beyond a "blood related" kinship group, beyond a community of common descent. Political citizenship however was not yet fully separated from the traditional consanguineal concept of legitimacy. In those early times membership in a political community was still fused with religion, common religious rites that were tribal in their nature. Foreigners were not admitted to the religious community and cults.[29]

Early Roman citizenship was also limited to the native tribal community, integrated by religion and religious cults. However, a tendency toward inclusion of allied tribes, toward absorbing the outsiders, appeared in the early stages of Roman history. Here were the early beginnings of a future universalistic tendency. The inclusive trend was not a result of an early definite policy, much less an early universal philosophy; it was rather a consequence of the practical Roman genius, of their skill to resolve problems in a pragmatic as well as orderly way. The institution of citizenship evolved and broadened as a consequence of practical (although at times forced) way of "conflict resolution." It was not generosity or humanity that set this sense of direction.

Romans were usually ruthless in their conquest, as were others, and their rule—when opposed—could be cruel as well. The victors did not help the defeated, as the Western Allies did after World War II; they did not feed and clothe them, but they sold them into slavery. *Vae victis* was the adage: Woe to defeated. The in-group sentiments were strong and rooted in religion, symbols and rituals; equally strong were the feelings of hostility toward the outsiders—if not outright hostility at least indifference. Foreigners did not have the right to marry Romans or to own land.

But, here was an institution that offered a road that cut through the walls of hostility and mistrust. It offered a road toward a free life, offered rights next to duties, in a word a privileged life in those oppressive and brutal times. And this institution was Roman citizenship which, within four or five centuries of its advance, was eventually extended to all free inhabitants of the Roman universal empire. This universal tendency was articulated by the legal concept of citizenship and the genius of Roman law, the genius of Roman jurists who made this law, the people who adopted and observed it in their writings, philosophers and rhetors like Cicero, who understood and interpreted the law to others.

This single institution extended a more humane atmosphere and protection not to all, true, but to the free—who were neither born in the city of Rome, nor were even of Latin or Italic origin but who inhabited a territory under Roman authority.

The Roman city-state, its territory, *Ager Romanus*, was not directly aggrandized by conquest of other nations, at least in theory. The new states were not absorbed into the Roman city-state, writes Fustel de Coulanges. What was extended was Roman power, *Imperium Romanum*, Roman authority and power. The conquered peoples did not join Rome *in civitate*, in the Roman Republic, but *in imperio*, they were subject to Roman domination.

The Romans practiced, however, diverse forms of domination. Theoretically at least, there were two major types of extended domination. One was complete subjection of conquered peoples (they became subjects *dediticii*); the other was an alliance (*foedus*) and members of the allied nations became *socii*, associates, partners of the Roman people. The latter was an important device of Roman international policy as well as of Roman expansion. Romans expanded by way of alliances that Rome dominated, in its early history, by association with neighboring Latin peoples, *Foedus Latinus*. Latium submitted to Roman domination. "Romans exterminated half of those forty small nations which inhabited the area, they robbed some others of their land and the rest was accepted as allies," writes Fustel de Coulanges.[30]

When a subdued nation or tribe were given citizenship, citizenship was separated from the original tribal (today we could say) ethnic bond.

New citizens were not "ethnically" Romans: They were not of the Roman religion; in terms of their local cults and rites they were ethnically different; they did not belong to the Roman tribes or clans. Such citizenships were not given easily. But it was here that the crucial process of modern citizenship, a separation of the political from the ethnic, took place. Formally, the Roman city-state did not extend its borders. Rome remained what it was. In terms of Roman legal logic it was Roman power, *Imperium Romanum*, Roman domination that was extended, and with it Roman citizenship. Those who were not included were foreigners or enemies. Those who were not Roman citizens were not recognized (except for foreign visitors). Such was the value of Roman citizenship that without it a person was outside the law. Citizenship was a necessary opening to normal life and to the community.

In consequence, citizenship and the rights and protection associated with it, was strongly desired. Roman citizenship was highly valued; it was not an empty shell or only a symbol. It carried real privileges of freedom, protection by means of, law, respect and access to opportunities: "Latins, Italics, Greeks, later Spaniards and Gauls, aspired to become Roman citizens." They could keep their own ethnic identities, while acquiring the new political one: "All of those nations . . . entered the Roman imperium. . . . They worked hard to enter 'the Roman city', to acquire Roman citizenship, and after a long effort they all did,"[31] writes Fustel de Coulanges. Thus eventually all free men in the Roman Empire became Roman citizens. The extension of citizenship to all was a cumulation of a historical development, an act of transformation of a local urban institution into a universal one.

Alliances however did not immediately secure full rights. Thus the *socii*, the allies, at times revolted, demanding *una cititas*, citizenship, and appealed to the Roman Senate "that we are all called Romans" and again later (86–84 B.C.) citizenship was an issue.[32]

Citizenship gave to everyone his basic rights: the right to marry a Roman, to trade (*connubium, commercium*), commercial contracts had legal validity; it protected a person and his family in its dealings with Roman authorities. But it also involved duties, above all military service and participation in government, in various assemblies and courts—but again, it opened opportunities to various offices. Moreover, a citizen and his actions were protected by *ius civile*, Roman law, the law of the land binding all citizens. Hence, a citizen could take action in court.

With the initial extension of citizenship to Latin peoples, citizenship was separated from ethnicity. This process of institutional separation is characteristic of the development of Roman social and political institutions. It paved the way to the universal society Rome became in the declining years of the empire. Extension of citizenship to foreigners, to former enemies, separated the very legal-political institution from old consanguineal bonds, from its original tribal identity and from tribal sacral associations. This was indeed a fundamental change, a revolutionary change achieved by way of a long evolutionary process. In consequence, citizenship became a flexible legal instrument that could be extended to foreigners and also an institution desired by many alien peoples. Rome extended its *imperium* and domination granting citizenship, but it also successfully integrated diverse peoples, peoples of differing religions, origin, race and ethnicity, into a single world empire. Here were the historical beginnings of the civic state—a state of a new political bond and identity—whose major quality was detachment of political identity and bond from the ethnic. In tribal states all were fused.

Citizenship and Civic Bond: How It Developed in Rome

Rome developed a territorial-political form of citizenship in the declining decades of the empire, a citizenship shared by neighbors of diverse religions and ethnicity. It became a legal and political foundation of the modern democratic civic state as well as of pluralism. We have outlined the beginnings of citizenship in Greece where it was still associated with the consanguineal tribal tradition. In Rome, in a process of institutional separation, citizenship was shared widely and had a universal, even cosmopolitan, quality.

This transition from a common descent to a territorial bond was not an abrupt revolutionary one. Initially the tribal bond continued. It grew weaker, however, and slowly it was "depoliticized" and reduced to its natural, far more narrow lineage of common descent. The specificity of this transition was in its formation of a new, higher and broader bond of loyalty—a political not a tribal loyalty—as well as acceptance into the political community of individuals who had no consanguineal associations with Rome and did not belong to Roman tribes and clans. To the contrary, they were more often than not of different "ethnic" affiliation or descent.

This historical process came to its culmination with the *Constitutio Antoniniana* (about A.D. 212) that extended Roman citizenship to all free persons in the Roman Empire *civitatem omnibus datam*, "citizenship given to all." "Henceforth, a man was a Roman citizen because he was a free inhabitant of a civilized world."[33] This law has its historical momentum. It introduced a measure of equality before the law of all free persons; it suggested extension of legal protection to all free persons. Now, a *civis Romanus* was not necessarily born into a Roman family or even a Latin tribe. It was not anymore primarily a tribal or a kinship bond. A citizen was now a free person living within the borders of the universal Roman Empire of what was at that time the true *Orbis Terrarum*, the world. Paradoxically, this law was introduced in the time of Caracalla (probably A.D. 212), during the reign of a ruthless and cruel ruler who killed his own brother, plundered provinces and was eventually murdered by a *prefectus praetorio*, the head of the imperial guard.

The new bond, the political-territorial evolved on two levels: from the original descent and tribal system and it expanded by means of alliances, at first with the Latin peoples (*Foedus Latinus*).

The archaic Roman society was a kingdom ruled by Etruscan kings, but the basic social structure of Rome continued even after the abolition of royalty. The upper class was formed by an aristocracy and the lower by *Populus Romanus*, the Roman people. The real roots of society were in extended families. This was indeed the strongest bond.[34] Extended families were connected by kinship; they formed clans or *gentes*. Gentes met in *curiae* and in turn ten curiae formed a tribe. Archaic Rome had three tribes divided into thirty curiae.

The entire system was based on "blood relations" and common descent—hence, the bond of solidarity was in a sense "natural" and strong. This system did not differ much from Homeric societies, an association of families, phratries and tribes, which were unions of various related families.

The key element of Roman organization was the *curia*, association of clans. Related families met in curia headed by a *curio*. Curia formed an assembly that had its sacral function. It was also a popular assembly—suggests Alfoldy in his analysis of the Roman system—that decided public and legal matters. In case of war each curia mobilized ten equestrians (*decuria*) and one hundred infantry (*centuria*). A tribe consisted of ten curiae. The strongest bond of solidarity was however in the curia and curial system.

This organization has to be considered in terms of Roman society. To follow Alfoldy—it is estimated that in the sixth century, even fifth century B.C. what might be called the Roman nation was not larger than 15,000 people on a territory not much larger than 8 km in diameter.[35]

An important change took place in the fifth century B.C., a change that might have set the road toward the original Roman evolution of citizenship. According to Alfoldy, the tribal system grew weaker while social division into *plebs* (people) and *patres* (patricians) increased. This weakening of the tribal system facilitated the shift from a consanguineal-political bond toward the territorial-political anchored in the city-state. Weakening of the tribal organization continued with strengthening of plebeian class institutions. The Roman plebs created their own institutions as well as religious cults. The office of the Tribune of the People was established and the Temple of Ceres was built. Cults associated with the plebeians began; now they formed a sacral community of their own. The people of Rome also introduced their own meetings, *concilia plebis*, as well as their own leaders, *tribuni plebis*. The tribunes had the right to assist the people against the arbitrary actions of the magistrates (*ius auxilii*).

Alfoldy points to the general weakening of the tribal organization and bond. New institutions, new sacral cults were not consanguineal. They did reflect rather class solidarity: and division. Social divisions called, however, for a general institution and bond that would integrate the entire nation and correspond to fundamental political solidarity: the solidarity of all members of the city-state of all of Rome versus the outside world which was considered foreign and largely hostile. Also an institution was needed that would mobilize the entire community in times of various emergencies, that would moreover supply legitimacy of political power and validity to the law. The evolving institution of citizenship represented such a bond.

Those were initial steps and critical times of transition from a tribal-consanguineal organization to a territorial and political one. In a further change, writes Alfoldy, plebeians replaced the tribal division by one more favorable to their interest: "The gentile associations . . . were not abolished, but largely replaced, constituted on regional basis—four of them . . . corresponded to four regions of Rome. They were the *tribus urbanae.*" Hence tribes were now territorial administrative units and not solely associations of common descent. In territorial units, neighborhood of course is the major principle of solidarity. A territorial system was eventually well established. The tribal assemblies, since the new tribes were territorial, were not under as strong an influence of common descent groups as they were before.

This transition from consanguineal common descent to territorial administration was also parallelled by political reforms and affected citizen rights. A plebeian citizen had now a legal protection, and he could defend himself in the courts against the influential patricians. "Through the provision that every citizen had the right to a defender (*vindex*)," continues Alfoldy, "legal protection was secured even to the poorest weak."[36] Political and legal change was closely related to the social metamorphosis of Roman society, to the growth of an urban society, greater division of labor and the emergence of a craft and merchant class. It was also tied to changes in military strategies—to follow Alfoldy's analysis— to a greater role by the infantry with a plebeian military formation. Hence, the emergence of territorial solidarity and bond was not an isolated change. It was part of a general social, political and military development. It was, of course, a consequence of an emerging urban civilization and urban society. The kinship solidarity, especially one of extended family, did not disappear. The family and clients formed a basic bond of Roman society. However, the tribal bond grew weaker. The territorial-political identification and bond tied to citizenship became stronger and culminated late, after centuries, in Constitutio Antoniniana when every free inhabitant of the empire became a citizen.

Beginnings of a Federal System

In its early history Rome was surrounded by Latin nations. Eventually Rome and the nearby Latins formed a Latin Alliance, a kind of association that could be considered as some kind of proto federation, *Foedus Latinus.* A dual identity and concept appeared: those people had their own, we could say today, "ethnic" identification and, in addition, a Latin one. Incidentally, this dual identity must have existed for many centuries.

In the middle of the 1970s, while doing research in Italian villages, I visited a neighboring town in Campagna, an ancient Ferrentino. While I stood and observed the interesting arc of an ancient Roman gate, a young boy no more than 12 or 13 years old approached and asked whether I might be interested in an ancient Roman inscription. "Of course," I said. He led me through a narrow wooded trail to a rocky hill; and on a rock, to my surprise, I noticed an old Roman inscription, commemorating a consul who, as I remember, had brought this area under Roman authority. My young guide told me, not without pride: *"Noi non siamo Romani, siamo Hernici."* [We are not Romans, we are Hernici.] "We were conquered by Rome." This young Latin boy had three identities: he was from Ferrentino (a local one), he was a descendant of Hernici, and he was an Italian (Roman), of course.

There must have been many such Latin peoples in earlier times. Pliny lists fifty-three *populi* and points out that this was an alliance large enough to defend itself efficiently.[37]

Originally, there were small nation tribes tied together by language, religious cults and rudimentary political organizations. Very early on Latins developed a dual identity. They had a broad identity, *civis Romanus*, but at the same time belonged to their *Populus Latinus*, and eventually to their local town *urbs*, hence possibly even a third identity. In addition, all Latins were united by some common cults, common sacred places and perhaps by general culture. The original alliance, *Prisci Latini*, was an alliance of thirty nation tribes, *Triginta Populi*, under Roman hegemony. Nonetheless, the alliance was considered as an *isopolity*, a political system of equals, and cities and peoples conquered or associated became part of this *foedus aequum*, union of equals. Still, Rome had obvious supremacy. "Certain customs," writes Sherwin-White, "which a man has originally shared through his status as a Latin, began to be considered as privilege dependent upon residence within the territory of a given state, or as a corollary of duties performed for the state."[38] Roman generosity was quite uneven. They granted all the rights of the *foederati* (allied federalized peoples) to Tusculum, but destroyed the non-Latin Etruscan Veii.

Populi Latini enjoyed a mutual recognition of laws and rights. They shared *connubia, commercia et concilia*, the rights of marriage, contracts and assemblies, and this meant validity of marriage (in a sense intermarriage) within the entire Latin Union, validity of contracts. It was not only the right to trade but the right to make contracts with Romans, enforceable in Roman courts, according to Roman law and vice versa. With *connubium* and *commercium* goes hand in hand the right to contract a marriage with a foreigner, which would be upheld in a Roman court of law with full validity of testamentary power and paternity rights.[39]

Citizenship and Dual Identity

The basic change in the status of the Latins was in extension of citizenship rights. Roman citizenship in those cases was no more identical with the tribal consanguineal community. It was tied to a political system, to a territorial bond of all members of the state. Thus, in a gradual evolution citizenship and broader political identity was separated from the tribal and consanguineal community. The Roman *civitas*, citizenship, was extended now to the Latin *populi*. Extension of Roman citizenship resulted in dual, even broader, identities, which were not conflicting, but rather, were complementary, due to the Roman legal and philosophical interpretation. And Romans, at least some of them, were quite aware of those complex identities. It seems that not a few were proud of it and did not frown upon "divided loyalties." Cicero wrote in *De Legibus*: *"Omnibus municipibus duas esse censeo patrias, unam naturae, altera civitatis. Ut ille Cato cum esset Tusculi natus in Populi Romani civitatem susceptus est, itaque cum orta Tusculanus esset, civitate Romanus, habeat alteram loci patriam; alteram iuris."* [In all cities we have two fatherlands, one which is given by nature the other, the civic one of the state. Hence Cato born in Tusculum was accepted into the state of the Roman people, but according to his place he was Tusculanus of Roman citizenship, he had a different local fatherland and other according to law].[40] Cicero continues, however, that his republican (Roman) citizenship ties him to the republic (universal one) to which he must be dedicated, willing to serve, and even die for it.

Toward the end of the republic, when Latins were already well integrated into the Roman political system, it was quite evident for thoughtful Romans that a person has more than a single identity. Cicero expressed in those words the full meaning of Roman citizenship, as well as its dual nature. The "ethnic" bond and identity—the Tusculan—continue, while at the same time, another broader and political identity is also present in the hierarchy of values. The political bond with the Roman republic carries duties, responsibilities and sacrifices. Cicero says Cato, the great statesman and patriot of Rome, had two identities, and he does not question his Tusculan identity since this is "natural," obvious. Here the Roman political identity is clearly separated from the Tusculan of common descent.

Applied daily to current and practical problems the institution of citizenship becomes more flexible but also further detached from the original tribal and consanguineal association; an anthropologist may call this a lineage and descent system. In this flexibility appears the genius of Roman jurisprudence, that is, of Roman jurists and statesmen, as well as of the Roman people who accepted and observed the laws of the land. At the beginning, citizenship was a local-urban institution, limited solely to the members of a single city-state. Step by step, stage by stage, it was extended to once foreign, even hostile peoples. Already by the second century B.C. Latins could acquire citizenship in another Latin state or city by changing their domicile (*ius mutandae civitatis*). They had and applied dual citizenship.

Citizenship was an unusually elaborate legal institution with many ramifications. Thus Roman citizenship was bestowed on non-Latins, *Romani Facti* (made Romans); there was also citizenship without a vote, *civis sine suffragio*—a citizen without a vote residing in a different republic could still hold public office in Rome. Rome expanded in two ways: by a kind of federal process and association with other Latin urban republics or by conquest. This was rather a unique and contradictory process of close association, alliance and incorporation. With time, citizens of various city-states, city republics, were considered simply as Roman citizens although they belonged to separate republics, hence dual citizenship and multiple identification. *Civitas sine suffragio* facilitated dual citizenship, and in the long evolution of Rome created a political form that ended by embracing the whole Roman Universe.[41]

A Forgotten Historical Milestone

The essence of the Roman political and legal technique was the separation of the political bond and identity of the tribal consanguineal from the ethnic one—and creating (in this way, step by step, an imperial universal citizenship.

With the fall of the republic and rise of the Roman Empire, citizenship was also extended to various nations and tribes of different culture, languages, even religions. True, the imperial period marks the decline of democratic and republican institutions. On the other hand, however, in an unusual process of fusion of traditional republican institutions with the new imperial ways, citizenship was extended to the entire Roman world and became instrumental in securing a long period of Roman peace—*Pax Romana*. With the enactment of Constitutio Antoniniana (A.D. 212), when every free inhabitant of the Roman Empire became a citizen (*civitates omnibus datam*—citizenship given to all), Roman citizenship became almost a world citizenship, a citizenship of the ancient Mediterranean civilization.

The dates of battles and wars are more often than not considered as milestones of history. They often were. In terms of the history of civilization, in terms of a world safe for an individual, however, Constitutio Antoniniana seldom is remembered (if remembered at all) as a milestone. The great nineteenth-century historian of antiquity, Fustel de Coulanges, wrote about this decree:

> In a course of history, one does not meet a decree more important than this one: it abolished differences between the conquerors and the conquered, between the dominant and subject people (*peuples dominateurs et les peuples sujets*), moreover it erased a far older difference which the religion and the law established between the cit-

ies. Contemporary historians hardly recorded it. . . . Difference between the citizen and subjects grew weaker every generation.[42]

Now the political bond and imperial identity were separated definitely from the consanguineal-tribal and detached from ethnicity, even religion. Romans were all people, not only those of the Roman *urbs*, born in the Roman clans and tribes, but simply men who were free inhabitants of the empire.

Separation of Bonds and Identities

The modern civic state was a Roman invention. During the course of several centuries a state evolved, which was governed by laws enforced by a government and integrated by the institution of citizenship and not only by the tradition of common descent or tribal links. Legitimacy was complex. It was an empire rooted in sacral and religious lore, which gave legitimacy to the authority of the emperor. But citizenship was a basic bond that molded the shape and nature of the Roman Empire. Citizens were protected by law and in early times had a share in governing the state. With the expansion of Rome, citizenship of the city had been re-shaped into citizenship of the "state," of the dynamic Roman Empire. At the end of the republic citizenship was already extended to all of Italy. Once only a municipal Roman or Latin institution, a local urban institution, citizenship became a bond of the nascent multinational or multiethnic state.[43]

This historical process moved through a continuous, albeit slow, separation of institutions. It affected essential, ancient and established concepts and beliefs. Rome also separated public property from private. The separation of public property was an essential condition of good government. Of course, Rome did not have separation of powers in the modern constitutional sense. Nonetheless, the Roman Republic had a clear division of government functions somewhat akin to the modern concept. Executive power and military affairs were administered by elected consuls, judiciary functions, and praetors. The praetor division was guided by rule of law, civil law. At its inception, kinship and tribal solidarity was integrated with religion, sacral cults and the political system of the city-state. All three bonds and identities were fused: ethnic, religious and political. In a historical process, political citizenship split from the narrow tribal bond, from ethnicity, and extended to other, once alien peoples. Sherwin-White points out that citizenship, especially one without the vote, was an expression of a tolerant and broad approach to political assimilation of aliens and paved the way toward a world empire. Greeks, who may have invented the institution of citizenship, did not apply a political technique similar to the Romans, although Alexander the Great practiced a cosmopolitan, worldwide policy, encouraging interethnic "mixing." But this was different. Extending Roman law and citizenship to those who were different, who belonged to different nations or peoples, who spoke different languages and worshipped different gods, was a way of expanding and integrating the empire. Thus, Romans created a new identity, a broader social-political bond, and political technique for multinational multicultural integration.

This process of cultural "fission" continued and moved into the realm of religion. The Edict of Toleration of Milan and Rome (A.D. 311–312) granted equal rights and equal recognition to all religions and cults of the Roman Empire.[44] The magnitude of this edict appears within its historical context. The ancient state is fused with and integrated by religious beliefs and cults. The tribal and religious nature of society is projected into the political one. A member of an ancient state is also a co-religionist, participates in the same cults, practices the same rites. Religion is fused with the political organization, as it is today in a fundamentalist Islamic state. Constantine's Edict granted freedom of religion. It did not establish a dominant religion that granted minorities toleration, which in effect would be tantamount to a subordinated status vis-à-vis the dominant one. All religions were granted the same rights. This was not only a legal and political revolution, but also a truly cultural revolution, within the majesty of the law.

A Roman citizen could be Christian, Jewish, Mithraic or "Pagan," and at the same time Greek or Ilyrian. True, the Edict of Toleration did not last long, as Christian hierarchy and theology grew intolerant. Soon, a long period of religious persecution and intolerance made its historical entrance. But it was still the ancient Roman world in its declining years that gave mankind the first formal Edict of Toleration. It was perhaps the last symbolic act of this classic ancient civilization.

Roman Empire Building

Citizenship appeared and evolved in Greek city-states and in Rome. This was an urban institution, an outgrowth of native democracy, associated with nature and growth of the cities. It was not an institution of large and powerful empires, of extensive territories and populations. Neither a democratic form of government, particularly that based on broad representation and frequent meetings of the assemblies, as the Greek and Roman practiced, nor the institution of citizenship, in its early stage, were practiced in ancient empires that exercised their authority over large territories. The early states of Greece and Italy were city-states. In contrast, in the East, in Asia, but also in Africa, powerful empires appeared quite early—empires of vast territories: Egypt, Persia, Babylon, Assyria. The city-states—at least some of them—were the result of slow development of original tribal societies, of growth and union of villages, which Aristotle described in his *Politics*, when he wrote about Athens.

Some cities originated with conquest, but conquest was not the only way. They grew also from early tribal village societies, and some, prominent among them was Athens, associated with some neighboring villages. Here the will of the citizen was a source of authority, while both religion and the consent of its free citizens supplied legitimacy. But this type of government was feasible in a small urban society. It did not lend itself to imperial expansion as a means of integrating and administering many diverse nations or peoples. Until the time of Alexander the Great, Greeks were not empire builders. Greeks did not incorporate large territories into their city-states as Persians did. They often lived on islands and small peninsulas, also on the shores of Asia Minor and not in the open and unending spaces of the Asian continent. They expanded their trade and influence by means of colonies established in foreign lands. The colonies were Greek trading enclaves among foreign peoples, limited in their territory, with no ambition to subjugate the host country. They did fight among themselves but when comparing them to great oriental empires, it should be noted that their expansion and conquests were rather limited. A democratic political system of antiquity, as well as medieval times, worked relatively well only in small well-integrated communities.

Empires of the East grew in subjugation of vast and populous territories incorporated by force into the conquering (what was at that time) nation-state. Large territories were kept together by means of force, powerful armies and efficient bureaucracies while, next to direct use of force and coercion, deification of their rulers supplied an ideological support for autocracy and a kind of legitimacy. In time coercion evolved into a passively accepted tradition and submission was prompted by manipulation of fear and symbols.

Greek and Roman democracy was the fruit of an urban civilization and was not effective when applied to integration of large territories. Democracy was a local urban institution, not an imperial institution. Oriental rulers knew about one political technique in empire building— autocracy. Once the Greeks expanded beyond their Hellenic borders in an imperial advance, as was the case in the time of Alexander the Great, they did adopt some techniques of oriental despotism. But this was tempered by Greek philosophy and Greek ideas of cosmopolis.

Those two political systems, the urban-democratic (democratic in the ancient sense) and imperial-autocratic co-existed, but conflicts between them—such as between Greece and Persia—were frequent.

When Rome expanded beyond its Latin republican limits it fused its native democratic institutions with the autocratic-oriental. This was a strange fusion, noticed in new customs as well in dress and behavior. Emperor Aurelius Diocletianus (third century A.D.) was wearing Eastern silk robes in the oriental way, with visitors prostrated at his feet. But, in the Roman tradition, he used the ancient title of *dominus*.[45]

Roman institutions changed and so did the culture. But not all things changed. Roman law continued, as did the Roman institution of citizenship in spite of the orientalization of imperial power and administration.

The Romans did not invent or develop a new political technique to govern and integrate large territories. They too adopted, in a sense, the assimilated oriental model of a supreme ruler, the emperor. However, they fused the despotic quality of the ruler with Roman institutions, which protected the individual. The genius of Roman law continued. With their practical sense of government, they extended Roman citizenship and Roman law over vast territories and combined the two contradictory systems of despotism and citizenship. The Roman Empire was—in spite of its orientalization—different than oriental autocracies. The Senate survived in some form, as well as Roman law, and the surviving political institutions resulted in a kind of political, even cultural, dualism.[46] Those diverse institutions were integrated into a single workable system. They were fused and in this integrated form diffused over the entire Roman Empire.

Imperial Loyalty and Bond: A New Identity

Rome, in its long development, created a higher social and political bond, transcending the traditional and "natural" one—consanguinity, kinship, tribism. This was a fundamental change and historical invention, for citizenship was a new, legal and political instrument that could integrate diverse nations in a vast territory. The Greeks never advanced citizenship thus far. Greek citizenship was a narrow urban domestic institution. Moreover, Roman citizenship, not unlike U.S. citizenship today, was desired by neighboring peoples, especially the Latins, since it provided a kind of personal security and also extended political and economic opportunities. It accepted a foreigner into the community of Roman law, which was the law of free Roman citizens. It was Roman citizenship that was permitted to embrace this variety of nations or *populi* not as conquered and subjugated nations, not as *hostes*, enemies, but as an integral—and in terms of law equal, or near equal—association. The Roman multiethnic policy was not a temporary, ad hoc policy. With time it became a basic political principle. We read in Tacitus' *Annals* (XI.24) that when the Senate's new candidates were considered some senators vehemently objected to those who were foreign born (we would say today new ethnics), arguing: "Once our native-born citizens sufficed for peoples of our kin, and we are by not means dissatisfied with the Rome of the past. . . . Is it a small thing that Veneti and Isubres have already burst into the Senate-House, unless a mob of foreigners, a troop of captives . . . is now forced upon us."

Emperor Claudius forcefully answered with a lengthy argument referring to tradition and their past and glorious history. He spoke with conviction:

> Not only single persons but entire countries and tribes might be united under our name. We had unshaken peace at home; we prospered in all our foreign relations, in the days when Italy beyond the Po was admitted to share our citizenship. . . . Are we sorry that the Balbi came to us from Spain, and other men not less illustrious from Narbon Gaul? Their descendants are still among us and do not yield to us in patriotism. What was the ruin of Sparta and Athens, but this, that mighty as they were in war, they spurned from them as aliens those whom they had conquered? Our founder Romulus, on the other hand, was so wise that he fought as enemies and then hailed as fellow citizens several nations at the very same day. Strangers have reigned over us.

This is not a "sudden innovation," Claudius continued, but old practice and tradition.[47]

Defeated enemies were accepted by the victorious Romans—in many cases—as equals, not as slaves or subject peoples. This was not a policy of exception but a policy of equal civil and political rights. Claudius, like other Roman statesmen of broader outlook, had a full understanding of the very nature of this policy as a basic instrument in constructing a workable, tolerable and peaceful multiethnic state. Roman rule was still cruel in its gladiatorial games and toward some of the conquered. Those were cruel times. Roman policies, however, must be considered in a historical context, which again does not justify cruelty, but only records the past.

The nature of the institution of citizenship and the Roman legal system made the fundamental difference between oriental expansion, conquest and empire building and the Roman, in spite of orientalization of Roman legitimacy. Caesar or emperor, as in an oriental autocracy became a deity, a subject of religious worship and cults, but old Roman law and republican tradition continued.

Why Citizenship Developed in Greece and Rome

In terms of logic, scientific questions usually inquire about how things happen and what makes them work, but do not inquire about why they work. We suggest a hypothesis, a tentative answer. This time we ask "why." Why did citizenship appear in Greek city-states and in Rome?

To begin with Greece and Rome, as mentioned before, were *urban* civilizations, which grew slowly. Athens accepted foreigners and refugees, and Rome did the same with the Latin peoples.

The native population of a city may lack certain crafts and enterprising traders. Thus, foreigners with proper skills may be welcome (as they were in medieval times, when they were at least tolerated). They formed what might be called a "complementary population" since their skills and functions complemented the social-economic structure of the city-state. Metiks or foreign traders were *simply* needed in Athens; they had skills and professions Athenians could use.

Political refugees from other city-states, as was the case in Athens, might have even been accepted with sympathy. After a time, they were integrated into the Athenian community. Trading involved visits of foreigners, many who stayed longer and eventually settled, provided that they were accepted by the local population and rulers. For a ruler, their presence and economic means may have been attractive since they were a source of revenue.

There was, however, more to it. Athenians could make other choices and decisions. Romans could also choose other options. It was a matter of Greek or Athenian and Roman culture, wisdom of statesmen and the sometimes unruly assemblies, that Greeks and Romans adopted and invented this unusual institution as part of their early democratic system. This could not have happened without the support of the Athenian and Roman assemblies, at least without a limited popular support.

The original distribution of power—a consequence of the political system—had its impact too. The democratic structure suggested a certain balance of power that made it difficult to establish or reestablish a tyranical or despotic system. Later, however, republican institutions yielded to an imperial system backed by military power. There were other historical choices available, and the model of oriental despotism was not far away.

"Law and legal institutions," to quote Ihering, "are consequences of human thinking and decision. And so was Roman Law."[48] Legal institutions were not necessarily a simple and sole consequence of historical conditions and nameless and uncontrollable social and economic forces.

Citizenship developed as a problem-solving process. Athenians and Romans faced situations that called for decisions and answers. Decisions had to be made and options chosen. Once however a historical road was chosen, new conditions were created with every step and every change and a new social as well as legal development was initiated. New powers were distributed and soon—in those states where laws were enacted and enforced—new and relatively permanent institutions were built. Once a road has been chosen, it is difficult to turn back to the starting point. A new social-political reality was created, which has its own momentum, and a historical process was on its way.

Citizenship was a consequence of such a process of development, of pragmatic laws and decisions where new decisions were built on the foundations of earlier ones, and with time a certain tradition was created. Laws and decisions affected values and even the daily outlook of the people. This time citizenship was the fruit of intelligent, pragmatic law-givers and jurisprudents, perhaps a handful of them (of some we have historical records, others are forgotten). They understood the situation and met the challenge with proper answers.

This development was not the result of some nameless historical force, which pushed mankind into an unavoidable direction, uncontrollable by man. It was made by men who applied the genius of Roman law, who had those unusual talents and created the practical logic and flexibility of Roman jurisprudence.

Roman law was logical and pragmatic, problem solving—but its unusual quality was in the ways it was applied. Extremes of the law were avoided—according to the maxim *summum ius-summa iniuria* (to apply the extreme of the law means to effect extreme injustice). The law was applied in practice with restraint and moderation, even with self-discipline.[49] "It was a product rather of jurisprudence than legislation," writes Ihering. Jurisprudence was in this case a result of legal states-manship of the governing class.

The institution of citizenship was not a result of a theory a priori, a consequence of an application of a theoretical detached concept. It was a problem-solving, practical process. *Causa legis*, the cause, the condition that prompted legal decisions, stimulated working answers. But this practical spirit in problem solving also had the support of a logical and well-developed jurisprudence taught and advanced by scholars, judges and lawyers who had a philosophical commitment. The growth of Roman Empire gave strength to jurisprudence and laws, but on the other hand the growing appeal of stoic philosophy affected decisions. Stoics taught a philosophy of equality and freedom of all men and women, irrespective of their origin and status; all were spiritual neighbors and fellow citizens. They believed in the unity of humanity and the world.[50] Stoic philosophy, with its ideas of natural law and universal ethics enjoyed wide acceptance. Cosmopolis—a universal society—was a stoic ideal. After the enactment of Constitutio Antoniniana, Roman citizenship had a universal quality. It was close to what we would consider today world citizenship. This was, on the one hand, a result of historical conditions, and on the other, of practical law, jurisprudence and philosophy, which guided the political and legal decisions of praetors, magistrates, consuls and the political classes of those times.

The historical process of the evolution of citizenship in Rome took more than five hundred years. Adding the Athenian antecedent—it was more like eight hundred years.

The Roman Empire was the first state of free citizens, all of whom belonged to various nationalities, *populi*, and were of diverse "ethnicity" and religion. Some of the emperors were of non-Roman, even non-Italic origin, belonging to what we would call today "minorities." Citizenship was also an institution protecting individual rights, protecting persons against the state. "The source of this entire system," writes Ihering, "was the idea of personality. . . . The civil law—*ius civile*—recognized the independent will of a person."[51] Citizenship became, however, not solely a legal political concept. As in Greece, it was also discussed in terms of philosophy.

After the Fall of Rome, the Roman Empire continued in Byzantium. Inhabitants of Byzantium were Roman citizens, they practiced—and greatly advanced—Roman law. However, they spoke Greek and were of Greek ancestry, what we would call today "Greek ethnicity," belonging later to the Eastern Greek church. But they called themselves Roman and were Roman citizens.

By this time, citizenship was already a basic institution of the Western civilization, surviving also in Byzantium. This universal—rather than tribal kinship—bond was reinforced by a universal religion, Christianity, until the desire for power and riches prompted internecine conflicts and wars.

Citizenship was a historical, social invention. Separated from tribal bond in the course of centuries, it created unity of peoples diverse in culture, origin and religion, by means of a legal-political construct of a standard higher than tribal or ethnic solidarity and loyalty. It was welcomed and shared by large sections of inhabitants of the empire.

Citizenship and a Multiethnic Civic State

The institution of citizenship became a fitting legal and political framework for organizing states with a variety of nationalities into a multiethnic state, a civic state. It created a political device for unity in diversity, especially ethnic diversity; a unity that set limits to excessive coercion of a state. Citizenship by itself—as an abstract institution—does not suffice to build a democratic civic state. Its creation depends on the entire political system and political culture of the inhabitants. It functions within a tolerant democratic and rational state. Nevertheless, it is a major and a practical device in the construction of multiethnic states as an association of free citizens of diverse ethnicity. It rests on the development of dual or multiple identities: the political, civic and ethnic (and a corresponding hierarchy of loyalties) that reconcile identification with the state, and at the same time with a particular ethnic community. The nature of polity by consent has to be accepted, supported or recognized by a critical part of a political class, as well as politically active inhabitants. Moreover, even a small and violent minority may weaken, even destroy, unity by terrorist action. Excessive pressures by minorities or majorities may break it up. It is a subtle, sensitive construct, which in its democratic, contemporary definition calls for an appreciation of individual rights and a political culture rooted in concepts of personal freedom and ethical commitment—a general humanity.

The Romans built an empire on a broad citizenship structure. But there were also times of brutal conquest, slavery and untamed cruelty. The full contemporary philosophical meaning of democratic and humane citizenship developed later; it was a result of philosophical writings and above all political struggles of centuries to come.

After the Fall of Rome, the institution survived in the cities, which continued as communities of free men and women. The cities built the bridge between the culture of antiquity and the modern state.

NOTES

1. Henry Sumner Maine, *Ancient Law* (1861, 1863; reprint, Boston: Beacon Press, 1963), p. 125.

2. Aristotle, *The Politics of Aristotle*, ed. and trans. Ernest Barker (1942; reprint, London: Oxford University Press, 1965), p. 93.

3. Ibid., p. 89.

4. Ibid., p. 96.

5. Ibid., p. 40.

6. Philip B. Manville, *The Origins of Citizenship in Ancient Athens* (Princeton, N.J.: Princeton University Press, 1990), introduction.

7. Ibid., p. 206ff.

8. Peter N. Riesenberg, *Citizenship in the Western Tradition: From Plato to Rousseau* (Chapel Hill: University of North Carolina Press, 1992), p. 52.

9. Mogens Herman Hauser, *Demography and Democracy: The Number of Athenian Citizens in the Fourth Century BC* (Herning, Denmark: Falayet System, 1986), p. 5.

10. A. W. Gomme, *The Population of Athens in the Fifth and Fourth Century BC*, Glasgow University Publications, 28 (Oxford: Blackwell, 1933), p. 51. Gomme estimates 168,000 total population for Athens, Piraeus and environs. See also, A. H. M. Jones, *Athenian Democracy* (Baltimore: Johns Hopkins University Press, 1986), p. 79.

"The clearest and best figures for the population of Athens come from the end of classical period." According to Hellenistic scholar Ktesirles, at the turn of the third century B.C., the census reported 21,000 citizens, 10,000 metiks and 400,000 slaves. Raphael Sealey, *The Athenian Republic: Democracy or Rule of Law?* (University Park and London: Pennsylvania State University Press, 1987), p. 6.

11. Hauser, *Demography and Democracy*, p. 5. Sealy argues in a convincing way that Athens was a republic, under rule of law, not a democracy. "If slogans are needed Athens was a republic, not a democracy.

But slogans lend themselves to distortion. . . . The words are treacherous. The positive thesis is that the Athenians strove through centuries to achieve the rule of law." Sealey, *The Athenian Republic*, p. 146.

The definition of the term is however a matter of agreement; the content of historical terms is subject to diachronic modification. The term *democracy*—so it seems to me—has to be considered within a historical context, in this case as compared to Sparta, Carthage and above all to contemporary Persia. Aristotle defined Athens as a democracy, but Sealey's argument about the rule of law is convincing.

12. Manville, *Origins of Citizenship*, pp. 11, 173.

13. Jones, *Athenian Democracy*, p. 67.

14. Aristotle, *Politics*, Book III, Ch. II, p. 97

15. Taken from a translation in David Whitehead, *The Demes of Attica 508–ca. 250 B.C.* (Princeton, N.J.: Princeton University Press, 1986), chapter 1.

16. Manville, *Origins of Citizenship*, pp. 188–209.

17. Hauser, *Demography and Democracy*, p. 62 indicates considerable variations in the size of the deme. His estimates are based on the number of representatives (*bouletai*) sent to the assembly (*boule*).

18. Quoted by Whitehead, *The Demes of Attica*, p. 233.

19. Ibid., p. 231.

20. Ibid., p. 365.

21. Ibid., p. 185.

22. Manville, *Origins of Citizenship*, p. 193.

23. Fustel de Coulanges, *La Cité Antique* (Paris: Librairie Hachette, n.d.), p. 227.

24. Whitehead, *The Demes of Attica*, p. 67.

25. Manville, *Origins of Citizenship*, pp. 210–11. He also discusses the philosophical content of citizenship in his conclusion.

26. Riesenberg argues in a convincing manner that until the French Revolution (1789) citizenship was discriminatory and nondemocratic. Riesenberg, *Citizenship in the Western Tradition*, p. xviii. However, perception of democracy as a philosophy and political system changes also in time. See, for example, Henry Sumner Maine, *Popular Democracy* (1885; reprint, Indianapolis: Liberty Press, 1976). Maine defines democracy solely as a system of government not as a philosophy of egalitarianism, or relative egalitarianism and active participation of all citizens. Maine's views were rather conservative. What democracy is or is not in terms of its meaning is, of course, a semantic problem, a problem of definition. Nonetheless, in its early definition of Athenian democracy the term is associated with some kind of participation or control of the government by citizens, and citizens are defined in terms of a democratic government. This appears clearly in Aristotle's writings when he tells us that Sparta and Carthage also have some kind of identity one may call citi-

zenship, but citizenship in fact is associated with a participation of citizens in government in some of its major functions. Citizenship in turn is defined by democracy, by a democratic form of government, and, we may add, the rule of law. See also note 11.

27. "One fundamental distinction through much of antiquity that corporal punishment, public or private, was restricted to the slaves." M. I. Finley, *Ancient Slavery and Modern Ideology* (1990; reprint, London: Penguin, 1992), p. 93. The Greek economy, like the later Roman economy was a slave economy; large numbers of slaves were employed in mines and public works.

28. Riesenberg, *Citizenship in Western Tradition*, p. 52.

29. Fustel de Coulanges, *La Cité Antique*, p. 440.

30. Ibid., p. 448.

31. Ibid., p. 447.

32. Ibid., p. 48. See also Theodor Mommsen, *The History of Rome* (New York: Philosophical Library, n.d.), p. 289.

33. A. N. Sherwin-White, *The Roman Citizenship* (London: Oxford University Press, 1987), pp. 279–83.

34. Geza Alfoldy, *Social History of Rome* (Baltimore: Johns Hopkins University Press, 1987), pp. 4–12. Also quoted by Alfoldy, R. E. A. Palmer, *The Archaic Community of the Romans* (London-Cambridge, 1970).

35. Alfoldy, *Social History*, pp. 15–17; quoted by Alfoldy, A. Guarino, *La Rivoluzione Della Plebe* (Napoli, 1975) and E. Ferenczy, *From Patrician State to the Patrician Plebeian State* (Amsterdam: 1936).

36. Alfoldy, *Social History*, p. 17.

37. Sherwin-White, *Roman Citizenship*, pp. 8, 18.

38. Ibid., *Roman Citizenship*, pp. 23–25.

39. Ibid., pp. 32–34.

40. Quoted by Sherwin-White, in ibid., p. 154.

41. Ibid., pp. 38–61, especially pp. 42, 52, 58–61.

42. Coulanges, *La Cité Antique*, p. 455. Also note 1 in the same work on *Constitutio Antoniniana*.

43. See a brilliant essay by Ernest Barker, "The Conception of Empire," in Cyril Bailey, ed., *The Legacy of Rome* (1923; reprint, Oxford: Clarendon Press, 1962), p. 65ff.

44. Mario Attiio Levi, *L'Impero Romano*, Vol. 3 (Torino: Il Saggiatore, 1963), p. 1001ff.; also Jacob Burkhardt, *The Age of Constantin the Great* (New York: Doubleday, 1956), p. 362.

45. Harold Lamb, *Constantinople: Birth of an Empire* (New York: Alfred Knopf, 1957), pp. 14–15.

46. Barker, "The Conception of Empire," p. 7.

47. Tacitus, *Annals* (Complete Works), trans. by Alfred John Church and William Jackson Brodribb (New York: Random House, 1942, p. 241).

48. Rudolf von Ihering, "Entwicklungs Geschichte des Römischen

Rechts," *Der Geist des Rechts, Ein Auswahl aus Seinen Schriften*, ed. Fritz Buchwald (Bremen: Carl Schunemann Verlag, 1965), p. 375.

49. Ibid., p. 11ff.

50. F. de Zulueta, "The Science of Law," in Cyril Bailey, ed., *The Legacy of Rome* pp. 189–92.

51. Ihering, "Entwicklungs Geschichte des Römischen Rechts," p. 46ff.

3

CITIZENSHIP SURVIVES IN THE CITIES OF EUROPE

THE ROMAN PAST

Western civilization originated at the borderland of Europe, Asia and Africa—in the Eastern Mediterranean, the fruit of cultural contact and exchanges between peoples of Greece, Middle East, Asia and Africa. It extended later to the Western part of the Mediterranean and still later over large sections of Europe and the entire world. What we today call "Western culture" may be considered by some as a kind of a "social myth" or ideology. But it does exist, though difficult to prove, as a kind of "megaculture" that integrates many European nations and today extends far beyond the borders of Europe and the Americas. Moreover, it is this culture rooted in the concept of personal freedom which, not without strong opposition and protest, becomes the core of a still broader, emerging universal culture. Its essence appears in values and institutions that can be identified in all those nations and cultures, those ethnic groups that share what we could call the Western "megaculture"—civilization within which we find particular, different nationalities and cultures.

Citizenship is a major Western institution shared by many nations and connects centuries of European political and cultural history; the roots of this institution go back centuries to Greek city-states and imperial Rome. As advanced as it was in its general impact as humanizing institution, it appeared first in the slave societies of Greece and Rome, also noted for their cruel practices and ruthless wars. Contradictions within the same society, the same culture, are commonplace. But even in adverse conditions some institutions direct individuals toward a more humane form of existence, one that is less brutal, fostering mutual aid and protection of personal individual rights.

Society does not change evenly or simultaneously in all areas of life and activities. Within the same nation-state ancient and often cruel ways and customs may continue simultaneously with the advancing humane and milder tendencies and expressions. Nor does history move on a single homogeneous road toward progress. Citizenship in Rome evolved within the contradictions of wars, cruel games and orientalization of the Roman Empire. But this was also a time of diffusion and appeal of stoic philosophy among the educated as well as development of a unique, logical legal system.

Moreover, in a centuries long history citizenship became a major, fundamental political institution of Western civilization. It spans more than twenty-five hundred years of not only European history, but also Western history. Tied to the rule of law, citizenship is the institutional, legal foundation of human rights and of the protection of an individual against the arbitrary power of the state. It is the common culture and common set of basic values that unites mankind and makes us understand those who share it, as well as respect those who do not. Our citizenship, which is part of this common culture of today, was in Rome a well-defined and not only legal but also later a philosophical concept. In times of the republic (first century B.C.) Dionisius of Halicarnassus wrote: "Roman people choose magistrates, ratify laws and declare war."[1] In times of the republic, citizenship was associated with Roman democracy. It defines not only personal rights, but also duties. Citizenship was in fact—to follow Riesenberg's argument—a privilege in a community of diverse peoples, until it became universal. Moreover, the genius of Roman jurisprudence, that is, Roman legal scholars and philosophers, created a new political bond, which separated from the ethnic origin—and Roman solidarity tied all free inhabitants, into a single polity irrespective of ethnicity and religion. Another invention of the practical Roman mind was a kind of early confederal pattern, or the beginnings of it, combined with the early *Foedus Latinus*, Latin Union.

The confederation of diverse peoples into a single political body was unknown to the Greeks, although they practiced the politics of alliances for the temporary coordination of policies and temporary association. A higher political bond of free citizens, of equals before the law, and confederation, a union of diverse peoples under the same system of laws, were two Roman inventions that survived two millennia or more. The content has changed with time, of course, but still some essentials remain and continue, often reinterpreted, connecting generations and securing the continuation of a legal and political culture.

ROMAN LAW AND TRADITION CONTINUE

The test of the vitality of Roman legal order and citizenship appears in the historical fact that it survived the Fall of Rome and invasions of "barbarians," not to mention Huns, Lombards, Goths, Visigoths and many others. Most of them left little behind but destruction and their names in the chronicles of Roman, Byzantine or Lombard historians. Nonetheless this period of foreign invasions and dominations—more or less from the fifth to tenth centuries A.D.—and the rise of Christianity—are crucial in Western and world history. This is the time when European nations as we know them today were formed and solidified. It was the end of the ancient world, of the ancient political order, but its culture survived. Various tribes eventually settled and mixed with the local population. Roman civilization, not unlike the Greek, was primarily a civilization of the cities. In times of barbarian invasions the cities were in decline; some like Aquilea were destroyed, but many survived.

This was the end of the universal Roman state for the Romans, a disaster of historical magnitude. The invaders were not as large in numbers as it may seem by the magnitude of the events. Statistical data of this period are of course not fully reliable and precise; they are tentative and often hypothetical. Italy had probably 5 to 6 million inhabitants. The invading Ostrogoths, in all, can be estimated at about one hundred thousand. In addition, most of the victorious nations had a tendency to assimilate the Roman culture.[2] This cultural assimilation extended to many aspects of daily life.[3] Roman law did not disappear; it continued to be practiced among native populations, while the Germanic and other legal customs were also in force. The Longobards settled in many northern cities (e.g., Pavia, Perugia, Bologna), mixed with the local population and tolerated, even accepted, Roman institutions.[4]

In spite of a catastrophic political change the cultural unity of this large territory, which was once the Roman Empire, had not been completely disrupted. To the contrary, the trade in the Mediterranean basin, with its variety of nations, commercial connections with Western Asia and Northern Africa, continued, and lines of communication were active.

The disruption of this unity came about in the seventh and eighth centuries with the Moslem invasion. This time, it was an invasion of a vastly different culture and different and proselytizing religion—not prone nor willing to assimilate with those of a different creed. In other sections of the one-time Roman Empire and areas of Roman cultural influence, cultural unity in some form continued, which was even reinforced by this outside threat.

This continuity was kept alive above all by Christianity, especially by Romanized Christianity, rooted in Roman and Latin tradition and also by law and education, as Pirenne indicates. The church inherited the Roman Empire.

At times historical linkages of this continuity were unusual. According to Haskins only two manuscripts of the *Digesta* and *Corpus Iuris Civilis*, the basic texts of Roman jurisprudence, survived.[5] But the teaching of Roman law never disappeared. The Middle Ages, which are, more often than not, called our Dark Ages, have fathered what we call today academic schools. Our universities formed and evolved in an initially slow manner, but later, in the fourteenth and fifteenth centuries, in a rather rapid way and by diffusion.

By the eleventh century Roman law became a major subject at the University of Bologna (officially recognized in 1158). It was taught by a famous legist Irnerius, who is credited with introducing "glossing" of the legal text. The University of Bologna was at first only a school of Roman law. It was, however, a school famous all over Europe, and already at this time, in the early medieval times, it had a faculty of eighty.[6] Student bodies were quite large during those rather early times. Our modern universities originated in medieval times. As a matter of fact, the entire system of higher education had its beginning in those "Dark Ages," which were also "uneven." There were isles of enlightenment and moments of greatness during those times of intolerance, prejudice, cruelty and persecution.

The number of universities grew rather rapidly. In the twelfth century Europe probably had four to five schools that could be called universities by today's standards. By the thirteenth century there were nineteen to twenty; in the fourteenth century more than twenty-five and in the fifteenth century about thirty. In addition, there were *studia* that claimed the status of a university.[7] This was a time of revolution in European education. In those universities ancient philosophy was taught and Roman law was a major subject. That way—it can be assumed—citizenship was also a part of the lectures. Universities were key educational centers, and students were numerous—hence the civic tradition in some form continued in those schools. Moreover, as the tradition of Roman scholarship and institutions was also carried on by the omnipresent medieval Church, the memory of ancient legal institutions and citizenship was not obliterated.

Roman law and Roman tradition survived in vast areas of what was once the Roman Empire and diffused along the way to the young nations of Eastern Europe. The Roman legal tradition spread over Europe with a wide reception and adoption of Roman law. Reception of Roman law came to Germany by the end of the fifteenth century; some provisions ceased to be binding as late as the 1900s.[8]

THE CITY

The very institution of citizenship survived during medieval times, but its meaning in daily practiced life changed; it did not have its full legal majesty of the Constitutio Antoniniana. The term continued to appear in official documents and in the early period (eighth century): "Latins and Germans functioned as citizens in the classical sense."[9] Hence the old, territorial principle continued. Citizenship continued as a broader concept, not narrowly "ethnic" or "tribal."

But the institution itself lost its old paramount significance. Society had changed. It is now quite different than in the Roman Empire. With the advance of feudalism, rural, even posttribal communities prevailed, and the significance of the cities—with the exception of some Italian and early Romanized townships—declined. New institutions related to the feudal system were introduced; new identities and bonds were created or appeared in daily life. Above all, Christianity, a universal religion, created a new identity as well as a new solidarity. It was an identity higher in hierarchy of values than the tribal or consanguineal. Not unlike citizenship (which was political), religious identity was also distinct from ethnic-tribal: it was different, higher, and was institutionalized by the church hierarchy. For large sections of the populations, Christianity became a primary loyalty and identity, perhaps the strongest one, and it was universal, supratribal or ethnic.

The city continued, however, to be a religious community as well—*mutatis mutandis*—not unlike ancient times. Holy days were celebrated by the entire community and local deities were displaced by patron saints. The protection of patron saints extended over the territorial (not kinship) community. Inhabitants often carried the name of the patron saint of the city. Residents' providential concern extended to the city or village community limits, major signs of the faith in the providential powers of the patron saints which continue even today in village and urban communities of central as well as northern Italy.

The Holy Roman Empire stepped into the tradition of imperial Rome. A new social, economic and political system and structure—the feudal order—is fused with the survival of ancient traditions. In the cities, especially Italian cities, next to religious organizations, guilds gain a powerful influence. The entire economic life of the community, including banking, was organized into guilds. In a sense, the entire city was territorially structured by a system of guilds since members of the same guild inhabited the same streets or sections.[10]

Citizenship, however, was not a universal institution of all free inhabitants, as it had been in the Roman Empire. It was reduced—again as in the ancient Greek city-states—to an urban institution of city dwellers.

MEDIEVAL CITIES AND CITIZENSHIP

The government and political nature of medieval cities varied over time. They differed also synchronically in diverse countries; even the cities differed within the same country. There was not one single type of municipal government. There were also considerable differences between the various city republics of Italy. In the north, cities continued to exercise considerable and independent influence. Cities had strong identities and inner cohesion reflected in local city government and patriotism. The inhabitants formed a commune and were bound by an oath. "One act of outstanding significance . . . marked the entry on the scene of the new urban community. . . . This was the communal oath of the burghers. Hitherto they have been only isolated individuals, henceforth they had a collective being. It was the sworn association thus created which in France was given the literal name of commune," writes Bloch. Common religion, religious rituals and festivities reinforced the political and social bond. Solidarity of citizens appeared also in certain laws. Some laws of Florence, Perugia and other cities demanded active help and assistance from all citizens in times of emergency and need under penalty of loss of citizenship.[11] Strong urban loyalties appeared in such Italian city-republics as Florence and Venice, where the city, not the nation was called *patria*, fatherland.[12]

The medieval cities were not solely a continuation of the ancient Roman and Greek tradition. In the north the communes in Italy were probably the fruit of fusion of Roman as well as German institutions. Still Latin traditions formed the foundations of Italian cities.[13]

Cities, however, were islands of urban and civic freedom within the sea of feudal society, of landed nobility and half enslaved peasant classes. Most of the cities were not sovereign and had only limited autonomy. The supreme power over the cities was in the hands of the emperors, kings, counts and bishops. City communities, however, fought for their rights and were able to secure juridical as well as administrative autonomy in Italy, France, Germany, England, and other countries.[14]

Citizenship continued in the cities and this meant a share of government, personal liberty, active membership within an urban political community. This solidarity and identity extended to all members, all citizens irrespective of their origin and ethnicity. Whatever the provenance of medieval citizenship, its major ingredient was ancient, uninterrupted Roman tradition.

The burghers, inhabitants of the cities, were as free as citizens were in Rome. In the countryside, most of the peasants were serfs. The bourgeois "took for granted," writes Pirenne, "the authority of the territorial princes. . . . They merely desired a place in the sun, and their claims were confined to their most indispensable needs ... the most indispensable was personal liberty."[15]

Usually after a year and a day spent in the city fugitive serfs gained freedom. "The air of the city makes you free," was a German maxim ("Die Stadtluft macht frei"). The statute of limitation secured the rights of a fugitive serf and nullified the rights of the lord. "Birth meant little," continues Pirenne, "whatever might be the mark with which it had stigmatized the child in his cradle it vanished in the atmosphere of the city." The city, in fact, was the only place that secured freedom to a fugitive peasant, tired of servitude and oppression. It was the only escape. Once in the city, he was free. The charter of establishment of the commune of Saint Quentin (1151) declared: "It does not matter who he is, nor whence he comes. If he is not a thief, he may live in the commune, and, from the moment he enters the city, no one can raise his hand to him nor to do him violence." Pellicani points to the cities as a cradle of modern capitalism, for cities were seats of freedom and a market economy.[16]

Cities were communities of freedom and relative legal equality. The striking difference appears in comparison with the countryside and the manorial village. A serf, a peasant, could not even marry before he paid a special tax, nor could he marry a woman outside his village without permission of the lord, who also received part of his inheritance; a peasant was even obliged to grind his grain in the lord's mill.

In the cities as in ancient Rome, citizens had equal rights. However, many inhabitants were not citizens, and there were various classes of noncitizens. In addition to citizens—*cives*—there were permanent residents who paid taxes and had legal duties (*incolae*), next to temporary dwellers (*habitatores*), even subjects.[17] The laws, of course, varied, as did the concept or meaning of citizenship.

In Poland, where municipal law was often adopted from German cities, particularly from Magdeburg[18] the principle that the "city air makes one free" was often challenged by nobles. There were cases where they sued the city in attempt to "recover" fugitive serfs. For example, there was such a case when a noble, St. Koniecpolski, sued the city of Lvov (L'viv) to "return" as "his" fugitive serf Dr. Marcin Kampian, who was a burgomaster of the city, had a doctoral degree and was a city-born inhabitant; the noble asked to hand over his children too.

By the sixteenth century in the Polish Republic of the nobles further limitations on freedom and equality were imposed. By the seventeenth century the general spirit of toleration of Protestants and dissidents had also declined. At this time it was the crown, King Sobieski of Poland, who ordered the City Council of Cracow to respect the laws and the old traditions and respect the same full rights of citizens who were Protestants and dissidents.[19]

Cities fought back and defended the liberties they won. Relationships between the cities and the king were negotiated, and charters were agreed upon.[20]

But in spite of those variations in city charters concerning liberties the basic concept of citizenship continued and survived, although the laws varied: personal liberty, equality before the law, certain share in government, guilds of various strength and influence, as well as the territorial-political identity of burghers who often were immigrants, still were a part of communal solidarity. The city became now patria, not only in Italy.

What continued in the spirit of ancient Roman traditions was a broad territorial solidarity. A medieval city was not a consanguineal community of related clans and fratries. To the contrary, with the foundation of new cities, and many were founded or rebuilt in Eastern Europe, in Poland, after Mongol and Tatar invasions, many of the new cities were inhabited by immigrants who spoke foreign languages and were at times even of different religions. They gave the oath of allegiance to the city; now the city was their patria, fatherland. Their citizenship was not tied to their ethnicity; although foreign born, they were members of the urban community.

The ethnic bond and identity did not disappear of course. A German immigrant in Cracow continued to speak German at home, read in his native tongue, enjoy German dishes, but in the city he shared the common bond of solidarity. He might have been a Lutheran or Roman Catholic and a German, but at the same time he was a *civis Cracoviensis*, a citizen of Cracow, thus, he had three identities or even more.

This urban solidarity was rooted in neighborhood. It involved duties, mutual aid in times of emergency, duties to defend the city, participation in the local political government. In times of war—in some parts of Europe—defense of the cities was connected with the guilds. Since members of the guilds usually inhabited the same street, it was their duty to man the defenses of adjacent city walls and the guild tower.

In fourteenth-century Perugia, we find among the prominent citizens a doctor from the Netherlands, as well as immigrants from other European towns. In sixteenth-century Poland we find immigrant citizens not only in the capital cities of Cracow and Lvov, but also in Przemysl. One of the tests of the supraethnic nature of city identity was the oath of allegiance to the city, sworn in Poland not only in Polish, but also in German, Italian and Latin. Immigrants from various lands were, after the oath, duly inscribed as citizens into *Catalogus Civium*, Citizen Register, and enjoyed equal rights. In Cracow when a new citizen, Francis from Brescia, was sworn in using the Italian language for the first time in the history of that Polish city, it was noted in the register: *"primus in lingua itala iuravit"* (first gave the oath in the Italian language). Moreover, some citizens had dual citizenship. A citizen of Cracow, a successful

Italian craftsman or artist, after paying taxes to a Polish city, returned to Italy and assumed Italian citizenship.[21]

When looking back in history, one notices in those cities little of what we call today "nationalism." Solidarity as well as identity was tied to the local territorial community and to religion. As identity and solidarity was different, so was also the fanaticism that moved mobs, or was it? The scapegoats were now those who were of a different religion: Jews, Protestants in Catholic states, Catholics in some Protestant states. The Western world was often hateful and prejudiced, and discrimination and persecution were practiced and legalized by the church and state; it was cruel and unforgiving. Hatred was rampant and sometimes blessed by church hierarchy. But the ideas of toleration and religious freedom were also born here; and at the same time, a measure of toleration was also established early in many cities.

Jews suffered persecution in Europe for centuries; hence it was rather unusual that there was a case when the old Roman tradition of Constitutio Antoniniana was invoked by a jurist and Jews were considered Roman citizens, *cives Romani*, and their rights in this sense were acknowledged. The Florentine legist Aretinus (sixteenth century) argued against the distinction of citizenship by birth and privilege, and recognized, in the case of the Jews, equal legal benefits, in terms of Roman law.[22] In Florence, even if in an exceptional case, still, after almost one and a half millennia the tolerant tradition and balanced judgment of Roman law, the tradition of Roman citizenship survived.

By the time of the Renaissance, the concept of citizenship as an urban legal institution was well established and extended from the shores of the Mediterranean—where the tradition was always alive—to the Atlantic and shores of the Baltic and Vistula rivers.

As in the Roman Empire, citizenship was extended to foreign nationals and was not tied to a single tribal-ethnic community. Citizenship continued as a broad multiethnic concept and institution. It encouraged peoples of various nationalities and religions to settle in distant cities, live together, share duties and privileges. It was not a universal institution, as it once was in Rome. Jews, an ancient urban people, were excluded from citizenship. Still, the diversity of experience and skills, direct cultural contact of newcomers from different nations, enriched the cities and created the European culture. Local communal identities and solidarity were vigorous. Citizenship continued as a pragmatic political bond of individuals of various ethnic backgrounds, although the Christian faith was a condition of inclusion into the "commune."

Citizenship was an occidental institution as much as the very concept of the European city. The Western city was a political association of individuals, of individual citizens, burghers. The city was a distinct legal corporation, had its seal and legal identity and *public* property as distinct from *private*. The medieval city was also differentiated from the state, although the state might exercise sovereignty.[23]

Citizenship reappeared in medieval times and continued as a vital, political institution. But it was not universal, as in imperial Rome; it was a local urban institution. It was also limited to one estate, it did not embrace all inhabitants, it was rather a privilege than universal right of an individual. Nonetheless, the cities were springs of Western culture and civilization.

CITIES: ISLANDS OF FREEDOM

The cities of Eastern Europe owed their growth to immigrant craftsmen and merchants as well as to scholars; they were the source of wealth and culture. Some of those cities in Europe were islands of toleration. In some cases religious dissidents and foreigners were admitted thanks to a king's tolerant outlook or approval by sections of the ruling class. This was the case of Unitarians in Poland. Periods of toleration were short and unstable, as they were in France after the Edict of Nantes. But, the admission of Jews to Poland, at a later time readmission in England, may have reflected a broader, less discriminatory outlook. Foreigners were admitted to the cities and granted citizenship also, and perhaps more often than not, because their skills or wealth were needed. And admission at times invigorated the spirit of toleration, or—to the contrary—after a period of toleration could turn into active discrimination, even persecution of religious dissidents, Protestants and Jews.

In Eastern Europe, after the Tatar and Mongol invasions, when peace was restored urban colonization flourished. In the early medieval times in Western as well as in Eastern Europe new cities were built. Native populations in many cases lacked the necessary skills, even capital, essential to an urban community. Foreigners of various nationalities filled the gap, they "complemented" the natives with their skills and trades. The newcomers formed a "complementary population," with skills and knowledge essential to the life of a city. They were of a different ethnic origin, speaking often different languages, although Latin was a universal language. They often belonged to different churches.

With the late Renaissance, at the end of medieval times, the situation had changed.[24] New cities did not mushroom. Although the process of assimilation took its usual course, it was not complete, and the differences in many cities continued. In the meantime, the native burghers learned skills from the newcomers or accumulated capital; competition between the "natives" and "foreigners" generated tensions and antagonisms. This was especially the case for the Jewish inhabitants who suffered various measures of discrimination. In earlier times, the Jews were a typical "complementary" population. They were often welcomed when their skills were needed; they "complemented" the yet absent crafts and trades people and filled a need of an urban community. But, there were also tensions and conflicts between the upper classes, the rich burghers and those in power and the less privileged journeymen and workers. This was not a world free from social and economic tensions and conflicts of course. Citizenship by itself could not offer a full answer in times of strong religious hostilities, bigotry and fanaticism. Nonetheless, the Roman tradition served European cities and culture well during medieval times and later.

ON FALSE BUT EFFECTIVE AND HUMANE THEORIES

Some political theories are not true or valid, and still exercise a powerful and sometimes benign humanizing influence on history.

Laws protecting individual freedom and basic democratic institutions were guided and prompted by a theory that was logical and convincing but had no support in fact, in anthropological or historical data. This theory—that the early state has been formed by voluntary agreement—social contract—is not validated. There is no evidence that humankind ever lived in such a splendid paradise. Still, we profit from its benevolent and powerful influence throughout the ages; it had a humane impact on the life and fate of millions of men and women all over the world who never heard about it.

Its roots can be found in Greek philosophy, in the stoic world outlook and writings that had an impact on Christianity and were reflected in Judeo-Christian ethics. But the creed of natural law was also a part of the general tendencies of humanism.[25] The theory affected also the development of the modern civic state and the renaissance of a broader concept of citizenship that was its foundation. This theory had also resulted in a convincing argument of the right of the people, of the citizen, to revolt against an oppressive prince, a theory that was vigorously proclaimed and discussed by the French Protestants after the bloody massacre of the night of St. Bartholomew.[26] The theory of social contract and natural law affected Western political thinking since the late medieval times, but its most influential and fruitful period came in the seventeenth and eighteenth centuries.

In a rough, general form the theory of social contract might be reduced to a rather simple story. In ancient times, people lived happily—all were free and equal; the supreme sovereignty at this time belonged to individuals who formed families. The initial civil society—and also a state—was the fruit of a legal transaction, by which previously free and equal individuals had alienated their rights of sovereignty in favor of a state they had themselves created.[27]

In this theory, not a nation, nor a tribe nor a family, not a group—but an individual—was the source of sovereignty and authority which he voluntarily transferred to the state. Hence the relevance of theory in terms of a person, an individual. It shifts the essence of political association from the collective to an individual. Thus, the basis of civil society and the state is, in using this approach, a contract of individuals—and the state is only a consequence of the legal transaction and will of individuals, of citizens. Edmund Burke, a prominent eighteenth-century English statesman, in his essay *A Vindication of Natural Society* (1756) stresses the superiority of this "natural" society of social contract over any later form of government. The theory is logical and convincing, based on reason and deduction, but there is no evidence, no historical verity or scientific validity, in Rousseau's famous volume on social contract.

This theory, which in terms of facts is false, was not only influential but above all humanizing and perhaps one of the most beneficial political theories in the history of mankind. It has fostered equality before the law, individual liberty, government by consensus of the governed; it guided the authors of the Declaration of Independence, the Bill of Rights and U.S. Constitution, as well as philosophers of the French Revolution.

Hence, two sources were present at the rebirth of the contemporary, modern civic state: the philosophical fantasy of social contract, general theory of natural law, and the pragmatic legal Roman system of citizenship.

Theory and philosophy, however, gave way to support of a general principle of government by consent of the will of the people, a principle that is sound by itself, in a sense self-explanatory, and is indeed a necessary condition for the exercise of elementary freedoms of an individual. It is a principle that is reasonable and fundamental by itself.

Historical evidence does not reach the very distant past when human society appeared in its most primitive form. Social anthropology does not offer any evidence of an early meeting when a social contract was written or stipulated. Early society, if we can call that way traditional, was closely interwoven with religious belief. The closest concept to an original "social contract" in the formation of the state was that free association of Greek communities. Historical city-states already had slave populations.

A social contract was a way, however, to calm the fears of an unknown future republican system that had not yet been experienced by a living generation. Those philosophers simply said, "This is not new, it is a very old system, it worked and made people happy." This look into past was needed to convince authors and listeners or readers. But above all it formed a strong legitimacy of government.

It is necessary, however, to distinguish the historical, empirical nature of the argument from the ethical one. In a historical sense the natural law theory, a benevolent philosophy, may find no support in an empirical verification in historical facts. So much of history was written, as Thomas Huxley put it more than a century ago, with claws and blood. But it may be, and is for many of us, ethically valid. It corresponds to our ethical feelings of justice and compassion.

Man may and does invent, however, new social forms and ways that are just, benevolent and workable that were not practiced in the past. In traditional societies changes in culture are opposed. Even a minor change of a ritual, of a symbolic gesture, meets with adverse reaction and is considered sinful. It is a quality of our culture that we recognize legitimacy of change. We accept change, at times with reluctance, even opposition and criticism, if we feel it is wrong. Change as an idea is part of our Western culture, but change by itself is—in our culture—not an evil or sin. Greek philosophy recognized and accepted change as "natural" (natural meaning part of nature in the Hellenic sense) since the times of Heraclit from Ephesus (sixth century B.C.). Greek philosophers suggested political change—change of the form of government. On the other hand, man is fearful of the unknown, and change is tantamount to an unknown future. We are ambivalent while rightly cautious, even inquisitive, about the nature and quality of change. Hence a philosopher may say, "It was tried before and it worked." He may say so to reassure himself and perhaps dispel our fears. He may say so guided by subconscious, latent and now manifest sentiments. Philosophers and leaders of the French Revolution referred to the ancient past and history.

The idea and theory of government by consent can be traced again to the fourteenth-century writings of Marsilius of Padua (as well as earlier predecessors). In his *Defender of Peace*, he recognizes the will of the people as the only legitimate source of political power. The Paduan scholar opposes the church's claim to legitimacy and exercise of political power as conflicting with the nature of state and society. The consent of the citizen is the sole source of authority and legitimacy in exercise of laws and business of government.[28] Two years after the appearance of his work Marsilius earned the distinction of papal condemnation.

The theoretical and philosophical tendency toward a future civic state continues. Three centuries later, Johannes Althusius rediscovered the federalist principle as a way of a free union of citizens and diverse territories by means of a free consent. He might have been inspired by his contemporary Switzerland and Netherlands. Althusius wrote about "a symbiotic association," "a community of men living together and united by real bonds, which a contract of union, expressed or implied, institutionalizes." He sees the way of political life as a way of "pactum"—agreement—"the bond of contractual union."[29] Citizenship is now tied to the very concept of legitimacy, which derives—in those theories—from the will of individuals. Legitimacy is not divine in origin, but is the fruit of an agreement, a social bond.

Hence, the concept of citizenship matures again and reappears in learned discussions and histories. When Leonardo Bruni, a fourteenth-century Florentine humanist wrote his *Laudatio Florentinae Urbis*, a *Panegyric to the City of Florence*, he extolled liberty and relative equality of its citizens. "Nowhere else does freedom grow so vigorously and nowhere else are rich and poor alike treated with such equality. . . . From this arises the saying that has been directed against the more powerful citizens when they have threatened the lower classes; in such a case, a member of the lower class says: 'I also am a Florentine citizen.' "[30]

Humanists taught the Renaissance generation dignity and appreciation of life and work of an individual, of a burgher, of a secular way of life. The mentor of Bruni, Coluccio Salutati, was an early protagonist of the superiority of an active secular life as opposed to the contemplative life of monks.[31]

During the Renaissance and later, the Western image of an individual, a free person and modern citizenship, is shaped by humanism and theories of natural law. It is an image rooted in classic Greek and Roman works of philosophers and historians and in contemporary political and juridical writings. Philosophy of the new positive civic identity was to a large extent of Italian making.[32]

The idea of natural law grew in relevance—political rights of citizens, the government by consent, liberty, equality before the law—all those basic ideas were legitimized by widely taught theories, opening the way for a powerful impact on the future, on the eighteenth century.[33]

This benign theory of social contract and natural law had also a universal quality. In its very broad sense of humankind it was more inclusive than the very concept of citizenship, which at that time was reduced to urban living.

The medieval concept of citizenship was a narrow one, limited to one estate, to the burghers, and to the cities. The theory of natural law restored this institution to its Roman, symbolic, universal meaning. This universalism could of course be traced back centuries ago—it did not appear out of nowhere.

Universalism was a part of stoic heritage and Christianity. It paralleled, however, the enlightened ideas of Renaissance humanism, which was moved by philosophical curiosity and search for a common heritage, common ethics or creed, even broader than Christian universalism. Pico della Mirandola searched for and believed he discovered a community or unity of ideas and ethics not only of great religions, but also of ancient philosophers in his "Oratio on the Dignity of Man" (ca. 1486), which he never delivered due to papal intercession.[34] Pico was not alone; he reflected his times and humanist philosophy.

The new and powerful philosophy of sovereignty of an individual, his dignity and his rights, later defined the eighteenth-century concept of citizenship. It gave to this—at that time medieval—urban institution, a quality of universal liberating ideas. Supported by theories of natural law and social contract, it was carried into the seventeenth and eighteenth centuries by the leading political writers of Europe, particularly of Britain and France, also Italians, who espoused a variety of political shades. Their work affected not only the text, but also the wording of the Declaration of Independence as well as the documents of the French Revolution such as the Declaration of the Rights of Man and Citizen.

With the declining years of the eighteenth century, the very concept of citizenship, its legal definition, became a fundamental institution of the nascent democracies and future civic states. Moreover, its philosophical essence of equal rights for all free persons irrespective of race, religion or origin under rule of the law, was well suited for the building of the multiethnic states of our times.

NOTES

1. Quoted by Peter N. Riesenberg, *Citizenship in the Western Tradition: From Plato to Rousseau* (Chapel Hill: University of North Carolina Press, 1992), p. 81.

2. Henri Pirenne, *Mohammed and Charlemagne* (New York: Barnes and Noble, 1992), p. 37ff.

3. Ibid., p. 139.

4. Riesenberg, *Citizenship in the Western Tradition*, p. 101ff.

5. Charles Homer Haskins, *The Rise of Universities* (1923; reprint, Ithaca, N.Y.: Cornell University Press, 1957), p. 7.

6. Gabriel Compayre, *Abelard and the Origin and Early History of Universities* (1893; reprint, Westport, Conn.: Greenwood Press, 1969), p. 29.

7. Ibid., p. 49; also Marc Bloch, *Feudal Society*, vol. 1 (Chicago: University of Chicago Press, 1970), p. 116ff.

8. Rudolf von Ihering, "Entiwicklungs Geschichte des Römischen Rechts, *Der Geist des Rechtes* ed. Fritz Buchwald (Bremen: Carl Schunemann Verlag, 1965), p. 3.

9. Riesenberg, *Citizenship in the Western Tradition*, pp. 102–103.

10. Edgecumbe Staley, *The Guilds of Florence* (1906; reprint New York: Benjamin Bloom, 1967).

11. Bloch, *Feudal Society*, vol. 2, p. 354.

12. Riesenberg, *Citizenship in the Western Tradition*, p. 151.

13. The origins of the communal organizations of the cities are difficult to trace back. Historians of the nineteenth century carried on unending and inconclusive discussions as to whether the beginnings of those associations were Roman or German. One of the schools of historians argued that the medieval communal organizations were only a continuation of Roman municipal institutions and traditions, while the other maintained that these were German institutions and legal forms.

See Jan Ptasnik, *Miasta i Mieszczanstwo w Dawnej Polsce* (Cities and burghers in ancient Poland, in Polish) (Warszawa: PIW, 1949). In chapter I, "Italian and West European Cities in Medieval Times," Ptasnik reviews differing views and theories of this controversial issue.

14. Henri Pirenne, *Economic and Social History of Medieval Europe* (New York: Harcourt, Brace, 1937), pp. 50–52.

15. Henri Pirenne, *Medieval Cities* (1925; reprint, Garden City, N.Y.: Doubleday, 1956), p. 138.

16. Henri Pirenne, *Economic and Social History of Medieval Europe*, p. 65ff. Luciano Pellicani, *The Genesis of Capitalism and the Origins of Modernity* (New York: Telos, 1994), pp. 134–38, esp. chap. 6, pp. 129–46. The literature on Italian city-republics is, of course, very extensive: to begin with the classic and voluminous J. C. L. Sismonde de Sismondi, *Histoire des republiques italiennes du moyen age* (Paris: Treutel et Wurts, 1815–1818) and the substantial and detailed monograph of E. Staley, *The Guilds of Florence* (1906; reprint New York: Benjamin Bloom, 1967). Sismondi appeared also in a short edition in English, *History of the Italian Republics* (Peter Smith, 1970).

17. Ptasnik, *Miasta*, p. 243ff., Riesenberg, *Citizenship in the Western Tradition*, p. 156.

18. Stanislaw Estreicher, *Krakow i Magdeburg* (Krakow, 1911).

19. Ptasnik, *Miasta*, pp. 243–44.

20. Riesenberg, *Citizenship in the Western Tradition*, p. 115.

21. Ptasnik, *Miasta*, p. 253.

22. Riesenberg, *Citizenship in the Western Tradition*, p. 156.

23. Max Weber, *The City* (Glencoe, Ill.: Free Press, 1958), pp. 88, 96–99. Also Pirenne, *Medieval Cities*, p. 153ff., and Pellicani, *Genesis of Capitalism*.

24. The long period of the Renaissance is difficult to establish in terms of "from-to." However, the historical time of the Renaissance of Western culture is not solely an arbitrary definition by historians. Historical periods do not have clear cut time frontiers; the history of culture is a process, usually fused or parallel to other different developments and processes. The continuity of Western, Hellenic, Roman and Christian civilization was never totally disrupted. So the Renaissance is a part of it, a part of a historical continuity. Nor are the Middle Ages all "dark" and cruel. At times of "darkness," one finds "bright" spots and men of learning, culture, communities and nascent universities. The sharp chronological divisions are arbitrary decisions of historians. The beginning of the Renaissance may be traced to the late twelfth and thirteenth centuries— its end period as far as the early days of seventeenth or late sixteenth century. For a long time, two or more historical periods were parallel although opposite, and each in conflict. The divergences and disputes led sometimes to the stakes and torture chambers of the Inquisition.

25. On the very meaning and ethical concepts of humanism; Paul Oskar Kristeller, *Humanizm i Filozofia* (Humanism and philosophy, in Polish) (Warszawa: PAN, 1985). This volume contains selected chapters and papers of Professor Kristeller published in his *Humanistic Movement* (1955) and *Renaissance Thought and Its Sources* (1979) and two symposia: *Chapters in Western Civilization* (1965), *Il Risascimento nella Storia del Pensiero Politico* (1979). On humanism see: Eugenio Garin, *L'Umanismo Italiano* (Bari: Laterza, 1964); E. Garin, *Scienza e Vita Civile nel Rinascimento Italiano* (Bari: Laterza, 1965); Pierre Mesnard, *Il Pensiero Politico Rinascimentale* (French ed. 1951, Bari: Laterza, 1965), vol. 2, p. 162ff. and of course a library of publications and monographs.

26. Mesnard, *Il Pensiero Politico*, vol. 1, p. 523.

27. Otto Gierke, *Natural Law and Theory of Society: 1500–1800*, trans. and intro. Ernest Barker (1930; reprint Boston: Beacon Press, 1957), p. 102; see also Barker's introduction, especially section 3, "Law of Nations," p. xxxiv.

28. Marsilius of Padua, *The Defender of Peace (Defensor Pacis)*, Trans. and intro. Alan Gewirth (1956; reprint, New York: Harper, 1967), originally written in 1324. See p. xxx of Gewirth's introduction and Discourse Two (chap. 4).

29. Johannes Althusius, *The Politics of Johannes Althusius, Politica Methodice Digesta atque Exemplis et Profanis Illustrata*, Trans. and intro. Frederick Carney, preface by Carl J. Friedrich (1603; reprint, Boston: Beacon Press, 1964). See p. ix of Friedrich's comprehensive and analytical preface.

30. Leonardo Bruni, "Panegyric to the City of Florence," and the introduction of Ronald G. Witt, in B. G. Kohl, Ronald G. Hirt, Elizabeth B. Welles, eds., *The Earthly Republic, Italian Humanists on Government and Society* (Philadelphia: University of Pennsylvania Press, 1978), p. 173.

31. Coluccio Salutati, in ibid., p. 90; also his "Letter to Peregrino Zambeccari," p. 93ff. See also note 25 above.

32. Riesenberg, *Citizenship in the Western Tradition*, p. 218. Riesenberg argues, however, that interest in citizenship declined in France and England during the Renaissance.

33. Gierke, *Natural Law*, introduction of Ernest Barker, p. xli.

34. Text of the oration in Ernest Cassirer, Paul Oskar Kristeller, John Herman Randall Jr., *The Renaissance Philosophy of Man* (1948; reprint Chicago: The University of Chicago Press, 1956), p. 215; see also P. O. Kristeller's introduction.

4

UNFOLDING OF DEMOCRATIC CITIZENSHIP

INVENTION OF CITIZENSHIP

The world's great civilizations, such as the Greek, Hellenistic, and for a shorter time the Arabic, affected not only one or a few nations but also entire portions of mankind. Civilizations extended in time and space do not grow in isolation, separated from creative meetings with other cultures, with peoples of different languages, customs or skin colors. Dynamic cultures of universal appeal, widely diffused over this globe, had universal quality and grew by means of meeting with "others," neighbors or distant travelers, who came to trade or to learn, by communicating, exchanging and borrowing.

The truly "racially pure" were and are only those few, singularly isolated peoples of primitive and traditional cultures. Contemporary culture, not unlike the Hellenistic one, is the fruit of the fusion of cultures and diffusion of cultural innovations; we could even say they are the cultural "products" resulting from those curious and enterprising individuals who were willing to dine and talk and eat at the same table but who had a different cultural heritage.

The same is true about our social and political institutions that secured individual freedom and human dignity. Citizenship is one of the fundamentals of the modern democratic state. It is a kind of political invention of a historical scale. With all the shortcomings of comparison or analogy between entirely different cultural products—artifacts and institutions—the invention of citizenship—the fruit of a gradual process could be compared, in terms of its magnitude, to the invention of the wheel.

Few historians indeed acknowledge its historical relevance. Fustel de Coulanges, the prominent French historian of antiquity of the nineteenth century, was one of the few who stressed its paramount significance.

Its beginnings are obscure, but the crucial point was the breaking of the umbilical cord between tribe and state, kinship, the consaguinal bond and in the case of Greece—a city-state. The initial step toward separation of the state from a fundamental kinship organization was taken in Athens. This was a local development—not a universal extension of this principle, which took place much later in Rome. Nonetheless, in Athens, so it seems, modern democratic citizenship was invented, in its initial still communal form.

The new historical stage of this institution was set by Rome, with the proclamation of the Constitution Antoniniana, which made citizenship a universal institution of all free men of the empire, irrespective of religion, ethnicity or personal or philosophical preferences. Stoic philosophy, which became at this time in Rome, the creed of many educated people, with its belief in the dignity of man, had probably also made its contribution to the universal nature of *Civitas Romana*.

Civic institutions declined with the Fall of Rome, albeit they survived in a truncated form in the Italian cities and diffused later to other European towns. It was a "truncated" institution, since it has lost its general universal character, being limited to the inhabitants of the cities. It was a privilege of city dwellers rather than a general right of every member of the state. Still, some elements of its past universal nature survived, since citizenship could be acquired by foreigners (today we would call them ethnics) who settled in Italian or other European cities; however, as a rule, only Christians could acquire this privileged status.

Independently—not necessarily from the Hellenic or Roman tradition—civic tradition of a protodemocratic nature as well as broad legislation of political rights originated with Germanic and Anglo-Saxon customs and institutions. Not unlike our entire culture, modern citizenship is also the fruit of intersecting and later mutual influence, fusion and diffusion, of different European cultures and peoples. It is the fruit of the creative dialogues of neighbors and visitors, a consequence of a meeting and acceptance, not of isolation and narrow traditional tribalism.

English, also British political institutions grew from a continuous effort and struggle not only of the nobility, but also of other classes of the English people to limit the power of the king (and furthermore of the state) vis-à-vis the individual. The paramount role of Parliament was also shaped by this struggle in which individual rights of a citizen protecting his freedoms and privacy—both personal and territorial—were firmly established. Parliament played a major role in the development and very formulation of political and human rights that today form the essential content of modern citizenship. The very symbol of citizenship in England and later in Britain did not acquire an ideological quality, as in France at the times of the Revolution, and free men and true citizens continued to be called "subjects."

During the dawn of Enlightenment, the French "philosophers" discovered the nature of a free government from the English model. Montesquieu and Voltaire, next to an entire school of writers and philosophers, educated the nascent political classes, making known the workings of British government, discussing the nature of free society, individual political rights, toleration and merits of a representative government. Next to classic Greek and Roman traditions and models, British contemporaries suggested the ways of new political virtues. The ancient Hellenic and Roman tradition and symbols, the British and U.S. experiences have been fused with the personalistic and individualistic philosophy of the French Enlightenment into a powerful political ideology, expressed in the 1789 Declaration of the Rights of Man and Citizen. Here, in France, in this creative fusion, the quest for a new and free society was articulated and popularized by means of symbols and rituals, social myths and political semantics. But it was not only Enlightenment that affected the advance of individual political and human rights.

The new symbols and philosophy also have early roots in the Renaissance. The Renaissance, next to its revival of antiquity and awakening of native culture and tradition, carried the ideas of the universality of mankind, and for some, like Pico de la Mirandola, of all mankind, Christian as well as non-Christian. The teachings of the humanists rediscovered again and again the value and dignity of man. Of course, we could move even further back in time. Every forward or backward step of our civilization has its antecedents.

Thus, the revival and the new definition of citizenship and rights of man, its new meaning, was the fruit of a cultural and historical confluence beginning with its early sources in antiquity. Citizenship, like other major cultural products that mark the road of great civilizations, is the fruit of the fusion of many traditions and cultures, of many nations and even historical periods. Here is its strength and sources of universal appeal. The result of this integration of Hellenic, Roman, Italian, French, British, Swiss, Dutch, as well as other contributions, makes citizenship, and later the civic state, a unique, originally Western institution, with a dynamic quality for worldwide diffusion.

Citizenship paved the way toward full emancipation of an individual from the fetters of the late feudal system and eventually slavery. It became a simple symbol and credo—that all men are equal before the law. From the myth and poetry of natural law grew the belief that since all men are born equal, no one is above the law. In our century, democratic citizenship became one of the safeguards against the omnipotence of the government and the state.

THE CHANGING DEFINITION: CITOYEN/BOURJOIS— FROM CONFUSION TO A REPUBLICAN DEFINITION AND IDEOLOGICAL SYMBOL

The meaning of citizenship, its very definition, was changing with time. And even today its core is still changing. Our political terms are of course associated with a corresponding political systems and institutions, which are an outgrowth of the entire political culture. While institutions and systems change, terms continue to be reattached to a new situation while realities are quite different from the past. The term *citizenship* has however a unique story reflected in its meaning in spite of numerous changes. Not all institutions change in equal path. Moreover, in various historical periods, diverse institutions changed in different ways. Take Rome as an example: Some of the republican institutions, among them citizenship, survived, even expanded under the Roman Empire.

After the fall of the Roman Empire some Roman institutions were either assimilated by the conquerors or simply continued. They were vigorous and strong enough to survive and continue even during and after the barbarian invasions, revitalized in medieval cities and during the Renaissance. Italy was above all an urban society, a society of cities that expanded and controlled the rural areas. In medieval Europe, beyond the Mediterranean (with exceptions, e.g., Hanseatic cities and Flanders) the situation was reversed. Political power rested with the feudal lords whose economic power derived primarily from ownership and control of large rural estates.

Western antiquity was primarily a civilization of the cities, an urban civilization. Power and political institutions were tied to Athens, Sparta, Rome; religious exaltation and fervor, with their creative visions were bound to happen in Jerusalem, Bethlehem or Nazareth. Medieval feudal power and influence shifted to the lords, to the manor and the castles, to barons and landed estates, to the rural society, while intellectual life in search of a refuge survived in monasteries (e.g., Monte Casino). Cities survived, especially where they flourished for centuries, even new ones were founded. But, in early medieval times their political significance— with the exception of Italian city-republics—did not match the castles and manors. However, in Italy, the maritime cities began to play major roles, and while ancient scholarship survived in monasteries, it was revived and gained new, fresh colors in the universities, products of urban civilization.

The status of the term or title of "citizen" survived somehow and continued, especially in Italy. The very status of the term left rather interesting remnants in small Italian townships, which declined and became villages, in the—at one time—remote parts south of Rome, in Campagna and a region called in the vernacular "Ciociaria." In the late fifteenth century in such townships as Fumone, the inhabitants of the walled ancient castle towns called themselves proudly *cittadini* (citizen), in contrast to those living in the fields, called *contadini* (villagers). Although the latter were often in a better economic situation, *cittadini* in terms of status considered themselves, and perhaps were considered by others, as a superior class of people. In another township, included in the announcement of the death of an inhabitant, customarily printed and displayed at the church entrance and in some streets, the title "Citizen" was printed below the name of the deceased, as a kind of honorific title; the name of the city then followed.

In France, during the time of the Revolution, citizenship became the central ideological and political symbol. The French Revolution elevated the idea of citizenship to a fundamental republican concept, more—to a virtue. Now, its modern meaning had been diffused all over Europe (and later to other parts of the world) as a revolutionary republican symbol of emancipation and freedom. It had a different meaning than in medieval times or even during the Renaissance when it was confined to the cities and—with some exceptions—closely tied to the Christian religion. Later, again in times of absolutism, the term played a minor role, but did not disappear; it "masqueraded, assumed protective coloration," as Riesenberg put it.[1]

In the Swiss urban republics of Geneva, Calvin established a theocracy; citizenship here was associated with the ruling religion. A similar tendency appeared in other Swiss cities. The Netherlands at this time followed a far more tolerant path.[2]

In Poland, the situation was again different. Citizens of the cities were hardly included in the *sui generis* nobleman's democracy of the Polish republic. Nobility formed a substantial but also also a separate estate that elected the king and met in parliament. It was a highly privileged class, while the peasantry was reduced to the status of an oppressive serfdom. However, both Catholic and Protestant noblemen shared *sui generis* citizenship of this republic of nobles and disenfranchised peasantry.

In France, where absolute monarchy struck strong roots in the seventeenth and eighteenth centuries, there was—at this time—little interest in a discussion of a republican institution.[3] The concept of the "subject" of the sovereign was at times equated with and other times confused with the ancient meaning of citizenship. In learned discussions, however, a new political and philosophical meaning of citizenship had been slowly redefined to become a symbol of historical significance in appeals and programs of the French Revolution.

The absolute monarchy of France was of course quite different from imperial Rome or republican Italian cities where the term *citizen* had a legal and clear definition and meaning. Still, the term appears in various French dictionaries with a variety of definitions. The difference between *sujet* (subject) and *citoyen* is mentioned, but seldom defined in a precise way. Additional ambiguities appear in the use of terms of *bourjois* and *citoyen*. The English term *townsman* does not convey fully the French historical meaning of *bourjois*. The variety of definitions appear in the seventeenth- and eighteenth-century dictionaries, which at times differ substantially. Thus, in a dictionary of Richelet (1680) *"bourjois"* is more than citizen (quelque chose de plus que citoyen). *Citoyen*, he argues, is a long-time inhabitant and a member of a state who is obliged to meet certain duties. *Bourjois* is someone who acquired certain privileges due to his residence for a number of years. Thus, privileges form compensation for these "services."

But a century before, in 1576, Bodin commented: "In France with the exception of the king all are citizens, to begin with the *prince 'du sang'*, ending with a peasant." But two centuries later, in a 1773 dictionary we read: "In a Republic everybody is a subject, in a monarchy all are subjects with exceptions of the monarch."[4] And so the discussion continues for many years and confusion continues until it comes to the critical moment of the Revolution, which leads to the 1789 Declaration of the Rights of Man and Citizen.

France was a monarchy; the king was all powerful and the French were divided into separate estates. The political realities of the country were far distant from ancient republican traditions. But in the cities inhabitants were *citoyens*: the classic tradition continued in books, schools, universities, even daily life, hence the term continued even among theological writers. For Bossuet, a seventeenth century French theologian, we learn from Rétat's essay, Jesus was *un bon citoyen*.

The difference between a townsman and a citizen was blurred and confused. Finally, Jean Jacques Rousseau, a citizen of Geneva, hastened with an explanation of the basic difference between townsman (*bourjois*) and citizen (*citoyen*) in a footnote to his influential *Social Contract* (*Du Contrat Social*) (which appeared in 1762). "Frenchmen," he wrote "do not understand and confuse the term *citoyen*—citizen—with *townsman*—bourjois. Buildings, dwellings form the town, while citizens form the city." "Frenchmen," he continues, "confuse these two meanings and concepts, as well as the rights of a citizen with the virtue." "The title of *civis* (citizen)," he writes, "was never given to any 'subject' of any prince, even in ancient times. Only Frenchmen use this term freely (*tout familiarment*) because they do not understand its true significance, as we can easily see in their dictionaries, since they have no true concept (*veritable idèe*). . . . The true sense of this word has been nearly completely obliterated among contemporaries (*chez modernes*)." "The only Frenchman who avoided this mistake," continues Rousseau with approval, "is D'Alembert, who in his extensive article on Geneva clarified this essential difference"[5] D'Alembert had indeed a lengthy article on Geneva in the historical *Encyclopedie*. He wrote not only on citizenship; he bitterly complained above all that there was not a single theater in this republican but also dull Calvinist city.

The difference between the two concepts appeared clearly in Latin; it also reflected Roman legal and linguistic precision. It is the difference between *oppidum* (town—the physical nature of a township, buildings, etc.) and *urbs*—a community of citizens. Since even the authors of dictionaries, lexicographers and philosophers were confused about the very meaning of citizenship, the average inhabitant, the subject of the king was even more confused (or did not care indeed about verbal subtleties). The issue was not only an academic one, however, and was not without major historical significance. The word citizenship was to become a leading symbol in the vernacular as well as iconography and folklore of the coming revolution.

The difference between "subject" and "citizen" is however far more confusing and relevant than the linguistic subtlety derived from town and city. For Rousseau, who was raised in a republican city where the meaning of citizenship was derived from a political reality, it was not difficult to perceive the practical, daily meanings of the terms. In France, at that time, ruled by an absolute king, the difference was neither clear nor relevant. The political position, the rights and duties of an individual, derive from the political form of government. Our contemporary Rétat, after a century of confusion, interprets the two distinctions in a penetrating, simple sentence and in Aristotelian terms. The two terms, the citizen and the subject, correspond to two concepts of equality: on one hand, active and legitimate equality of the citizen, on the other hand, equality of all in subordination and dependence of the slaves.[6]

Returning to the age of discussion, to the eighteenth century, Montesquieu relates the distinction to the fundamental forms of the government. Montesquieu, in the footsteps of Aristotle, distinguishes three forms of government: a republic—where the entire people (*peuple en corps*) or part of it has sovereign power; a monarchy—where only one person rules, but within the limits of established laws; a despotic state—where one person exercises power carried out by his will and caprice but without any laws and rules. In a republic the people are a sovereign power, and this is democracy; when the sovereign power lies in a part of the people, it is called aristocracy. "The people in a democracy are—in a certain sense a monarch—in another one a *citoyen*." But he argues further, "in monarchies which are well governed (*réglées*) everybody will be almost a good citizen. . . . The love of equality dominates democracy, hence the only happiness is to render greater services than other citizens."

The terms *citoyens, sujets* and *peuple*, Montesquieu writes further, are usually associated with democracy—on the other hand *sujet*, subject, is also associated with monarchy and slave with autocracy. His sympathies for a democratic and republican form can be spotted easily; although, writing in an absolute monarchy, he is careful with words, even when he expresses the merits of the government of England this, *"republique qui se cache sous le form de monarchie."* Still, the use of the two terms is not clearly distinct. Even in a monarchy, Montesquieu would argue, some could be good citizens. Nonetheless, the author of the *Spirit of Laws*, frequently used the term *citizen* when writing about freedom, republic, democracy, sovereignty of the people. He argued that love of fatherland is associated with democracy, honor with monarchy.[7]

Three decades later, Holbach, not unlike two centuries before him Althusius, speaks about a government by consent of the governed. A government by consent is a government of the citizen. "The true citizens are also those of a legitimate sovereign who governs the people according to their consent, when the will of the head is a faithful expression of the society, hence a subject, obeying the laws which he approved, can call himself a citizen; he has one city [*citè*] one fatherland."[8]

Holbach is of course not an exception and not the first to discuss the legitimacy of power in terms of consent of the governed. The concept is of course a logical consequence of the theories of natural law and social contract. At that time, it had some practical application in England. Nonetheless, Holbach's theory was now a part of a broad discussion on government, shared by other *"philosophes."*

A process of desertion of intellectuals was already in progress. A characteristic symptom of an intellectual malaise or of a basic political change, related to a breakdown or revision of values, is the ideological or philosophical desertion of the intellectuals who once supported the established order. This sociological phenomenon appeared and reappeared in the European past. It also took place prior to the French Revolution, reappeared before the Russian Revolution of 1917, and again in the dissident movements opposing Soviet totalitarian rule. It is indicative of change, of revision of ideologies, a breakdown of belief systems and values, even collapse of a political or social system. In a milder form, it may occur when social and political realities are in striking contradiction with the governing ideology or legitimacy.

Rétat suggests 1750 as a historical watershed for this debate and intellectual change in France.[9] Around this time, the term citizenship was already defined and associated with the sovereign power of the people, and it appears in the company of other symbols: *patrie*, patriotism, virtue, happiness and particularly with the ideas of human and political rights. We shall limit this extensive debate (reported so well by Rétat) to two views, which are indeed relevant in defining citizenship on the eve of the revolution: that of Diderot and that of Siéyès.[10]

Diderot wrote an article on this subject in the famous *Encyclopedie*, which reflected the world-views of the French philosophers as well as the ideas of Enlightenment. Hobbes, wrote Diderot, is correct, when he makes no difference between subject and citizen. Both are "subjects": the former of the monarch, the sovereign, and the latter of the laws. Citizens are governed (*commandés*) by moral principles (*être moral*), a subject by a physical person. All citizens are equally part of "nobility" (*egalment nobles*) but the nobility of citizens derives not from ancestors but from laws. A citizen is both: a sovereign, since citizens govern, and a subject, since he accepts the authority, the rule of his government. In times of dissolution of the established system, a citizen accepts the cause of equality and freedom of all citizens. Diderot, however, sets limits to equality. "Even in a perfect democracy," he continues, "a complete equality of all citizens is a 'chimera' (*une chose chimerique*) and may become a way of disintegration." In Diderot's words, citizen is already defined as a sole source of sovereign power.

France before the revolution was not a single integrated nation. In addition to substantial regional differences it was divided into three estates: of those "who fight and defend," those "who pray" and last, the lowest, those "who work"; hence it was divided into nobility, clergy and townsmen. Peasantry was not included. Division of estates also carried a distribution of privileges. The peasants had none, nobility had the most, clergy was not far away. A society of citizens was one where all were equal before the law; whether a monarchy or a republic all members had an equal legal position.

A general, universal, national bond, with the exception of a common allegiance to the king, did not exist. The monarch was a supreme arbiter of a society divided into privileged and disadvantaged sections.[11]

France awaited national unification, undivided by a system of privileges. Emmanuel Joseph Siéyès, in his influential essay, *Qu'est que ce le Tiers Etat*, published in January 1789, addressed this important issue of the abolition of estates. Siéyès was not the first to address the issue of a nation, but his writings had an impact during the crucial days of the revolution. Siéyès advocated the abolition of estates and all privileges and the creation of a single nation of citizen. This was to come in August 1789.

Siéyès began his essay with three questions that could have been translated easily into a political program. "What is the third estate: Everything. What was it until now in a present order: nothing. What do we demand: it should become an active part (something) (*a y devenir quelque chose*)." Siéyès demands the transformation of France into a nation, an association of politically and legally equal individuals.[12]

By 1789, citizenship was closely associated with the "people" and patriotism, liberty and democracy; it became antinomy to aristocracy. Now, the terms and symbols of citizenship carried the basic ideas of the coming revolution, which was defined and redefined in the daily press and ongoing oratory, a positive symbol for the republicans and "patriots" and a negative symbol for the royalists. Its meaning and relevance culminated in 1789 when the final text of the Declaration of the Rights of Man and Citizen was voted on and accepted by the National Assembly.[13]

FROM A SYMBOL TO A LEGAL INSTITUTION: STAGES AND ROADS OF A POLITICAL CONCEPT

During the years before and during the French Revolution, this major symbol of freedom—citizenship—matured and spread widely over Europe and beyond. It grew with the rise of nationalism, as a part of it; hence it was not clearly separated from nationality, unlike the Roman institution. However, with the abolition of estates its medieval quality of an exclusive urban institution, in a sense a privileged one if compared with the peasantry, changed. Citizenship was extended to all; even the king was called citizen in pamphlets during the Revolution.

In a final and comprehensive democratic and republican definition, the concept of citizenship arises with the replacement of the three estates by the National Assembly and a declaration of abolition of privileges—a proclamation of equal rights for all. A single concept of legitimacy of power and loyalty now resides in the nation. Citizens are now the nation and not the king. It was indeed a historical moment, in August 1789, when—as the historian Thiers reports—"everyone hurried to the tribune, to renounce his privileges. The nobility set the first example."[14]

This was a complex process but its major stages, even if not entirely distinct, can indeed be followed. In its final stage citizenship was elevated to a major national institution and gained general acceptance and legitimacy. Interestingly enough, it was advanced and supported by some members of the aristocracy, to cite Siéyès and Mirabeau, who voted against their own personal privileged status. Citizenship was not only a vague subject of philosophical discussion and journalistic articles, it also became part of a new political reality. It was not only an ideological symbol but also a legal institution, a consequence and articulation of a nascent republic.

The long story of the revolutionary rebirth of this institution is of major interest. It tells us how a vague general term—not even fully defined— became a basic political and ideological symbol. It demonstrated how a symbol, in a rather slow process, is translated into political action, and finally into the law of the land and eventually into an important instrument of political change, into a legal and political reality. It was the journey of a symbol that moved from an appeal to action to political fact.

The renascence of this key institution of a civic state was mirrored in a long process that was not only a social-political reality, but also a semantic one, corollary to the advancing social and political change. It began in France: The very term and institution was vaguely defined in French dictionaries and philosophical discussions, albeit confused with other terms. At this early stage it was still a vague and general term, inherited from classic Roman and Greek tradition, sometimes fused with feudal and medieval memories of a particular, at times privileged, status of the townspeople of the Third Estate, which contrasted the highly privileged nobility on the one hand and subject peasantry on the other.

The second stage appeared with the growing intellectual and political ferment of the eighteenth century, with its dominant theories of natural law and social contract. It was also a time of growing interest in the working and nature of the English government, that "hidden republic" as Montesquieu called it—"*une nation ou la republique se cache sous la forme de monarchie*" (a nation that hides the republic behind a form of a monarchy). It was a time of Enlightenment, and clubs and discussion circles were mushrooming not only in France, but also all over Europe. As early as 1724 members of the Club d'Entresol, presided over by Saint Pierre, discussed British political institutions, and perhaps it was their enthusiasm that prompted the king's order and closed the club.[15]

The republican form of government and citizenship was also the subject matter of theoretical writings and discussions by the philosophers of the Enlightenment. In their discussions the term "citoyen" was defined as a positive norm and institution, associated with a free society. In those witty writings and learned discussions of the *philosophes*, this vague and ambiguous term known until now in its medieval and classic tradition, ripened into a positive and clear republican symbol of freedom and equality before the law. It was well integrated into republican ideology.

The third stage—the basic concept of republicanism and of course citizenship—moved from the "ivory tower" of the philosophers to the reading and debating public, to the mass media of the time: newspapers, clubs and public meetings.[16] Popular terms were coined in dailies, periodicals and pamphlets. Classic concepts and symbols were popularized; they descended now from the heights of the learned dictionaries and philosophical essays and debates to the street corners and piazzas as part of the new vernacular of active and dynamic politics.

Next we come to the fourth stage—when the idea of a state governed by representatives of men who enjoyed equal rights and were not divided by diverse status into privileged and subordinated, reached the legislators. Some of them, for example, Siéyès, fathered the new meaning of the term. In August 1789, all privileges and special laws were abolished and the rights of citizens were stated in a declaration that was to become law. It was indeed a long list of privileges that were abolished and new rights were proclaimed. Thiers, whose work was written during a time not far removed from those historical days, and whose memories were still alive, tells us:

The assembly has decreed:

The abolition of serfdom and the rights of compounding for signoral dues.

The abolition of signoral jurisdiction.

The suppression of exclusive rights to hunt.

The redemption of tithes.

Equality of taxes.

The admission of all citizen to civil and military employment.

The abolition of sale of offices.

The suppression of all the privileges of towns and provinces. . . .

The abolition of feudal rights has been agreed upon.[17]

A long historical process was needed to establish a modern republican citizenship, in other words to create a nation of members subject to the same laws. During this fourth stage the institution became an instrument of public policy, an instrument of change. This close connection between dynamic ideas and action was seized on by Giuseppe Mazzini, one of the fathers of the Italian *Risorgimento*, in his once famous appeal *"pensiero e azione"* (thought and action).

The law was not yet part of a daily, practical reality; it had to be applied and introduced to daily life. Implementation by means of propaganda was done again by the press, theater, education, and even cartoons.[18] The new creed of citizenship also created a new terminology, for example, *civique, civisme*. In a 1790 dictionary it was defined as: "a term invented lately to define a new virtue, probably unknown to the ancients."[19]

The return of the monarchy brought along with it strong criticism of republican concepts, symbols and philosophy, including the concept of citizenship. Joseph de Maistre argued about using this term, which became fashionable in France, when it was unknown in other European languages.[20] A subject became a clear antonym to a citizen who was defined as a member of a democratic republic.

THE FATE OF A SYMBOL

The term *citoyen* grew with the advance and enthusiasm for the revolution. It spread all over Europe and beyond with the republican creed and influence of Enlightenment and rationalism. After the disastrous year of terror its appeal declined, however, when what some historians called "reaction" set in. The daily appellation of *monsieur* returned and replaced *citoyen*.

Citizenship and democratic changes—the former being only its articulation—did not affect all aspects of life. Women were not embraced by the demands of political equality.[21] The National Assembly was ambiguous concerning matters of slavery, with some exceptions. Nevertheless, the French Revolution created a symbol that expressed civil liberties and the rights of man.

The Declaration of the Rights of Man and Citizen, which put down the fundamental philosophy of citizenship, had a wide and truly revolutionary appeal. The creators of this historical document used simple and direct language. To quote Mirabeau, who chaired the Committee of Five that drafted the document, "The authors have chosen a popular form (*cette forme populaire*) which would appeal to the people. . . . We did not use scientific and scholarly style, which one learns in school in abstract thinking. . . . It is the way . . . Americans have done in their Bill of Rights, they have avoided science (*ils ont . . . ecartè la science*). They presented political verities in a form which can become easily one of their own people."[22]

Thus the French Enlightenment and the French Revolution revived the universal meaning of *civis*, citizen, *citoyen* and created a political symbol of equality and freedom of unusual appeal. Its message was written in the words of the Declaration of the Rights of Man, although the full emancipation of all had not yet happened. But this historical declaration destroyed the legitimacy of slavery, justified so easily as an institution of biblical tradition.

It also affected the humiliating inequality of women. Furthermore, it challenged the serfdom of the peasantry, which still survived in large parts of Europe, as well as discrimination of Jews and other religious minorities. The new democracy recognized government by consent, by the will of the citizen, as the only source of legitimacy and political power. It was a universal citizenship, open to all. Eventually it was instrumental in terminating the ancient traditional connections of slavery, discrimination and privilege for the ruling minority of nobles, Catholic clergy and privileged few.

THE ENGLISH, BRITISH CONTENT OF CITIZENSHIP

The National Assembly did not invent citizenship, as historians may argue.[23] Athenians and Romans were the real inventors and early practitioners of the concept. The Romans contributed the legal framework and the logic of the institution; they made it a universal institution of a world empire, separated citizenship from ethnicity or tribalism and later (in a historical context) religion. European cities contributed the essential historical continuity, tradition and humanistic colors of the Renaissance— the dignity of man, the dignity of a person.

But the British, more the American-British, contribution was at the very essence of its eighteenth-century meaning as the pragmatic content of the concept, the basic value of individual and political freedom, spelled out in a clear and convincing way in terms that could be and were translated into the practice of daily life. Modern citizenship was, to a large extent, an articulation of a legal and political system they invented, the fruit of a long historical development preceding or concurrent to the history of both nations.

As Mirabeau, who chaired the editorial Committee of Five stated, the committee followed the American example even in style. The Virginia Bill of Rights, the Declaration of Independence, the U.S. Constitution, the English political system were not sole antecedents of the French document but also influenced French and political philosophy and ideas. The American impact on the French Revolution, especially in its early democratic stage, was of course substantial.[24]

The English influence came through the writings of Montesquieu, Voltaire and other "philosophes." Classic ancient Greek and Roman input as well as American ideas were audible and visible in the halls and piazzas of the revolution, as well as in publications, discussions and numerous clubs.

The French contributed dynamic and appealing ideology, they infused the wisdom and the wit of the Enlightenment and Rationalism. They created the iconography, songs and music: the "Marseillaise," with its appeal to *citoyens* became an emotional call and anthem not only for France. Early on Mirabeau saw the universal nature of the appeal, of ideas and reforms, when he said: "Our laws will become European laws, should the nations of Europe earn this dignity. Your work (on Rights of Man and Citizen) will extend to our grandchildren, to the entire world." Mirabeau's words carried a universal message.

French citizenship was an instrument of unification of France; it contributed to the creation of a French nation. At this time, when patriots spoke about French people or the French nation, they meant the inhabitants of the French state who at that time spoke a variety of distant dialects and were also divided by provincial-cultural differences.

But was citizenship universal in France in the same way the sense of citizenship was in Rome? The historical situation was of course entirely different. It was universal and had some similarities to ancient Roman practice.

France at the time of the revolution was not a single, "monolithic" nation, with a single culture. There was no single language accepted and recognized by all, and the differences of what we call dialect, and what may amount to a different language, were substantial. The French Convention had difficulties in propagandizing the new republican creed. The broadminded and tolerant Abbé Gregoire was entrusted with the difficult task of translating the major documents of the republic into coherent and easily understood languages. According to Braudel, his report, after careful study, has shown that, "The French did not only have the languages of ole and oil (not to mention more or less foreign languages of the outer periphery of the Kingdom, hence Basque, Breton, Flemish dialects, German), but almost an infinity of patois." The dialects were quite different and not easily understood.

Braudel cites Gascon as an example, which was different from Languedoc or Provencal. Gascon on one side of the river Garonne spoke a different *patois* than was spoken on the other side of the river. A correspondent wrote to the abbé about the difficulties of translating "the revered Declaration of the Rights of Man."[25] French citizenship reinforced or possibly created a broader French identity, after local identity. For provincial identity did not disappear; it was expressed in everyday life, in the use of the vernacular, even in local revolts. It was not too different from the early republican period of Rome, when local identity of Latin cities was complemented by the new identity of the Roman citizen. Citizenship had an obvious appeal to people in the provinces since it abolished all privileges; it was extended to all inhabitants who met the elementary conditions as well as to all classes or estates. In this sense, it was universal.

Unlike imperial Rome, however, citizenship from the beginning was associated with French nationality, with French culture. Unlike Rome, where Emperor Claudius (as well as some historians) took pride in what we would today call "ethnics," nationals of different ethnic origin were a part of the Roman community of citizen, patriots were Frenchmen. The state was identified with nationality. But French national identification was broad and inclusive.

Whatever the differences, the Roman Empire was not the only historic model of a civic state, and it was not a democracy. The French Revolution, in spite of its sanguinary interlude, created a modern national—but also in a context of time—a historical period of a civic and a tolerant state, a model others would soon to follow or attempt to imitate.

However, other narrow tendencies soon appeared, adverse to the broad concepts of those early philosophers of nationality, for example Herder, who saw nationality, a nation, as a part of humanity. It was nationalism in its later, extreme form, that opened the gates of twentieth-century fanatic tribalism. The seeds of this trend however appeared toward the end of the eighteenth century when, according to Barberis, Barruel used the term "nationalism" in 1798–99: "Le nationalisme prit la place de l'amour general . . . il fut permis de mépriser les étrangers, de le tromper, de le offenser. Cette vertue fut appelée patriotisme."[26]

Nationalism—as opposed to the humanism of the Enlightenment—was the antonym of the universalism that appeared in the Roman Empire, which—in spite of its oriental and autocratic form—had assimilated civic qualities of the early republic. Nationalism appeared at the same time when, after more than one and half millennia, the civic polity was reborn.

Nonetheless, French philosophers and followers of the French Enlightenment were instrumental in the creation of a historical symbol with a powerful political appeal, articulated in poetry and art, as well as political theories, a symbol that carried the message of political freedom, equality before the law, human rights and above all the dignity of man. There was of course a hiatus between the idea and reality, between theory and daily practice. But—with all its limitations—it was a symbol of a human and universal quality.

MAJOR SOURCES OF CITIZENSHIP

Citizenship is more than a French creation; it is a European institution. Not one, but several European cultures, several nations, made essential contributions and supplied the building blocks. To begin with, the Greeks and Romans provided the name, the legal concept and political frame. They created a universal institution continued by medieval cities that during the decline of the Roman order and subsequent invasions preserved the term and the ancient Roman institution, later enobled by the Italian Renaissance. The idea, if at times vague and not yet well defined, inspired the French Enlightenment and created the very symbol, folklore, image and appeal.

The basic principle of modern government and representative government associated with citizenship (although without such appellation) was the fruit of British and later of American political culture through a long historical process. It was a fusion of all those elements, all those contributions, as well as other nations and city-republics that created this fundamental and humanizing institution. It is indeed a "Western" institution and contribution.

Neither the British nor the Americans elevated the term "citizenship" to a key symbol, an icon, as the French did. The French created an orig-

inal political folklore of the French Revolution. Its major hero was *"citoyen"*—an idealized, as well as an ideal type of new political man, a
wise, incorruptible and patriotic member of the republic, a man ready
to sacrifice his life for the new holy trinity: liberté, fraternité, egalité. The
solemnity and rituals of a religious quality were now projected into politics. *Citoyen*—for a time displaced *monsieur*: It was used in daily language and above all in official addresses and solemn meetings. The
British and Americans did not create this type of political folklore. In
England, in Britain, in spite of great political change, members of the
state continued to be called "subjects," although in the true meaning of
the word, they were citizens.

The Jacobin movement had a modest influence in America, and for a
short time, the French style affected somewhat radical American groups.
Some democrats in Boston addressed each other as "citizen" and ladies
as "citizeness"; later the nature of the English language shortened it to
"citess." British and the American philosophers and men of practical
politics, as well as the very polity, created the meaning, the very sense
of modern citizenship.[27]

BRITISH POLITICAL INSTITUTIONS

In the past as well as today, British political institutions served as a
model of a democratic, representative and parliamentary form of government. They are however of English or British origin not Roman der-
ivation. The same is true of English associations of townsmen
participating in the government of cities. (I suppose that in cities founded
by the Romans, such as London, there was some Roman urban influence.) British historian J. R. Green notes that the English borough was
originally a community with some rudimentary form of association
"whose inhabitants used to live together either for purposes of trade or
protection. . . . It is this characteristic of our boroughs," continues Green,
"which separates them at once from the cities of Italy which had preserved the municipal institutions of their Roman past. . . . But in England
the tradition of Rome had utterly past away, while feudal oppression
was held fairly in check by the crown."[28]

Individual and political rights form the essential part of the modern
concept of citizenship. They were won in England and Great Britain, in
a long process that stretched over centuries by way of bargaining or
through political struggles that involved the king, nobles, barons and
lords, the cities, the middle class, and later the crown and the House of
Commons. The roots of these freedoms did not originate from Greek or
Roman tradition, or from Italian institutions, which survived the barbaric
invasions. "For the most the liberties of our towns were bought in this
way," continues Green, "by sheer, hard bargaining. . . . The earliest Eng-

lish charters, save that of London, date from years of Norman wars, when Henry the First needed money for his costly Norman wars. Later money was needed for the mercenary troops."[29]

All kings need money all the time, and towns, hence commercial and industrial centers, had a rudimentary money economy. This was the place where money was. Townsmen were merchants, they bought their freedoms.

This was of course only part of the early story. Major developments toward individual, personal political rights took place later in a long historical period from the thirteenth century until the twentieth. But the very beginning of this long process of bargaining, negotiating and struggle goes back to much earlier times: to Saxon kings and their Grand Council. At first, the lords, who were great landowners, affected the power of the king by limiting his authority and winning rights for the nobles.

Gradually the power of Parliament was extended at the expense of the crown. With time the role of the House of lords diminished and the House of Commons grew more powerful and decisive. During this long process of bargain and struggle, confrontation, even civil war, a balance had been established between the diverse power centers, which facilitated the emergence and continuous extension of individual freedoms, civil and political rights.

The power of the "Chief Tenants," of the lords, kept in check the power of the king, while the king in turn checked the feudal demands for privileges of the lords. Later the House of Commons applied the weight of its decisions to check the power of both the king and the lords.

Thus, Parliament advanced from those early councils toward an all national representation. It was a long process with milestones, like the Great Charter of the thirteenth and fourteenth centuries, later statutes (e.g., the Bill of Rights of 1689), and nineteenth- and twentieth-century legislation, which led to universal suffrage. Unlike most of the European nations, England experienced the trend toward universal national representation of all free men early on.

Representation during those early times was neither universal nor equal; the poor, the villeins, were not yet in the House of Commons. But a trend was already moving in this direction. Moreover, enfranchisement, the end of serfdom, began in England relatively early, earlier than in most European states, and culminated in freedom by the end of the sixteenth century.

Concepts and institutions of political and human rights, essential in defining present-day citizenship, grew in England from native sources. "The Common Law, the great inheritance of the English speaking nations," writes Trevelyan, "has in modern times sharply divided them

in their habits of thought from the world of Latin and Roman tradition."[30]

Still Roman law and ancient history was studied in English universities. Nonetheless, philosophy of individual rights and personal freedom
was closely tied to native English institutions. Basic values, ancient institutions, attitudes and the entire political culture affected the development of a "political person," free and independent, and fostered the
forms of government with a parliament admired in Europe.

Parliament in turn was not the result of a single revolution nor a single
historical event. Parliament was not an institution imposed by force by
a winning political party. It grew and changed through centuries of political debates, conflicts, struggles and compromises. "The English people," notes Trevelyan, "have always been distinguished for their
'committee sense', their desire to sit round and talk till an agreement or
compromise is reached. This national peculiarity was the true origin of
the English Parliament."[31]

Not only theory or philosophy alone but also practical political techniques made British politics a well-working process, which had been
moving toward the extension of individual rights, while again and again
escaping the perils of tyranny. Here belongs the very concept of limitation of power (whether of the crown or later of the state), the skills in
applying compromise, even after a long conflict, the sense of balance of
power between various power centers of the realm.

The institution of individual and political rights has been advanced in
Parliament through a long process, interrupted—at times even frequently—by confrontation and civil wars. English civil wars led, however gradually, to the limitation of power of the crown and the state, to
the extension of individual rights and to the advance of religious freedom and toleration. In his *Philosophical Letters* of 1733 Voltaire wrote,
"Here is the most essential difference between Rome and England: the
results of civil wars in Rome has been slavery, the fruit of turmoils in
England, liberty."

Limitation of power of the Crown by which later individual, personal
and civil rights were extended, appeared early in English history and
was manifested in the Great Charter of 1215, a watershed in the history
of liberty. Nor had the king legitimacy of absolute power, as he did in
eighteenth-century France.

A prominent lawyer of the fifteenth century, Chief Justice Fortescue,
commented on the English constitution: "For the King of England cannot
alter or change the laws of the Realm at his pleasure. For he governeth
his people by power not only royal, but politique." And Trevelyan comments, "constitutional—as we should say." "In other countries of Europe," the chief justice continued, "based on Roman Law, the will and
pleasure of the Prince has the force of law."[32]

In England rather early, it was national representation in Parliament, where the legitimacy and authority had moved gradually to the consent of the majority of all free men, and the principle of government by consent had been slowly but firmly established. Things have to be considered, however, within the context of time. This was of course not yet a representation of the nation comparable to one based on twentieth-century universal suffrage. The British concept of legitimacy, in its historical development, was also closely associated with the principle of the Rule of Law, the principle known to the ancient Greeks, but again, in England it had its own native history and roots.[33]

The councils, which developed gradually into the houses of Parliament, also had an unusual continuity, essential in the development of legal institutions. Twentieth-century Parliament preserved a traditional and historical continuity from its thirteenth-century early political ancestry when the House of Commons was in its infancy. To quote Lord Acton: "The one thing which saved England from the fate of the other countries was not her insular position, nor the intendant spirit, nor the magnanimity of the people . . . but only the consistent stupid fidelity to the political system. We have had a civil war without proscription and a revolution without bloodshed. We have had our share in demagogues, but no one has succeeded in establishing tyranny."[34]

"Fidelity to the political system" was, however, far from inane; to the contrary it was rather a test of popular political wisdom. Continuity of an institution or of a political system is not necessarily always beneficial, it is not by itself a virtue. Dynastic Egypt and China had remarkable continuity, even stability, as did Persian autocracies and Russian tsarist rule. But here was a system that produced centuries of an efficient and workable Parliament, a particular kind of stability, unique in political history—one that advanced the cause of freedom and human rights.

In a long history of struggle for a better, humane society, change was and is of course essential, even imperative. But political as well as social change also calls for stability and continuity, so that necessary transformations and reforms can move within the firm and stable channels of permanent institutions. The breakdown of institutions, with ensuing radical changes of "everything" in society, within those few weeks of revolutionary fervor, caused dangerous moments of social anarchy and disintegration, which lent themselves to the establishment of new tyrannies and ended with an autocratic or dictatorial government, a government that consolidated power by terror and violence.

The parliamentary political mechanism, the ways of political conduct, were changing gradually but had a relative and remarkable permanence. Within the limits set by parliamentary ways and procedures an unrelenting historical process moved toward a society now governed by the will of many and toward individual and political rights for all. Ancient traditions and customs—which may have struck an outsider as strange and useless—contributed to this stability of institutions.

Not everything had to be changed concurrently. Wise conservatism was seminal not only for the conservatives, but also for reformers with radical points of view. During times of change the issue is—what should be conserved and what should be changed. The weakening of some basic foundations of a good society, the weakening of essential values, could be detrimental for the very existence, integrity, workability and betterment of a society. Within the walls of Parliament, with its strong legitimacy, views were exchanged and laws enacted that culminated in legislation that enhanced personal rights and individual protection against unrestrained power.

The beginning of English territorial representation goes back to the thirteenth century, when Simon de Monfort in the king's name ordered elections of four knights by each shire as well as two citizens from each city and two burgesses from each borough. The shires had been territorial units of local government, which had a measure of self-government. The boroughs too had self-government and elected their own administration.

In a historical process the two orders eventually associated formally as the House of Commons. This new connection of the estates welded the orders and created a unity and a representative institution. Thus, in this evolution, Parliament became not an assembly of separate estates but of two houses. Hence, the legislative activity of Parliament during an early stage affected the political history of the entire nation.

Nor was the House of Commons deprived of political power. From its early beginnings Parliament made decisions concerning taxes and grants. To quote Trevelyan, "Noble and commons, clergy and laity were made equal before the law of the land . . . the liberties of medieval clergy and aristocracy, slices of sovereignty held in private or corporate hands, were resumed in favor of the liberty of the ordinary English subject, sheltered behind the power of the state."[35]

During the twelfth century, taxes were assessed by a jury of neighbors, representatives of the taxpayers. In consequence the very concept of taxation and representation had been welded together. By the fourteenth century money grants and taxation were to be initiated in the House of Commons, and already by the fourteenth century, no tax could be imposed without the consent of Parliament. Feudal customs or laws secured for the lords a place in Parliament, as king's counselors, but the House of Commons was there due to the desirability and necessity of their agreement. Within the rule of law, the House of Commons step by step consolidated its control over the royal purse.[36] It had a share of necessary power to protect and further subjects' individual and political rights.

Other European countries, for example, Poland and Hungary, boasted of early parliaments. But the Polish *Sejm* was not a body of national representation; it represented the nobility and the clergy almost exclusively, issuing legislation that extended the nobles' rights and privileges and reduced step by step the entire peasantry to a servile status. It was a noble's republic; although in the fifteenth and sixteenth centuries there was wide toleration of religious dissidents, which was unique as Europe at that time was experiencing religious wars.

In sixteenth- and seventeenth-century Poland, religious and philosophical literature was the topic of numerous discussions and publications. Prominent among them were also publications of early Polish Socinians. At that time (before the Counter Reformation) the idea of religious toleration was influential among sections of the nobility and townsmen.[37]

During the golden age of the Polish republic of the nobles (which lasted about 150 years during the sixteenth and seventeenth centuries), the republic was indeed a kind of pluralistic and civic state of the privileged classes (of course within the context of that historical period). The nobility, a rather large social class and estate, accepted into its ranks "nobilitated" Lithuanians, Ukrainians, Tatars, Germans, Armenians and Belorussians. Ukrainians with dual identity (called Ruthenians) were identified by the formula *natione polonus gente ruthenus* (today's idiom of Polish nationality and Ruthenian [Ukrainian] ethnicity).

During the Diet (*Sejm*) and Confederation of Warsaw in 1573, when Europe suffered rampant and ruthless religious wars and persecutions, this meeting of the nobles recognized the concept of religious dissent and solemnly promised under oath not to persecute and discriminate against dissenters. They also affirmed a policy of religious toleration.

However, the treatment of the peasantry grew harsher and ever more oppressive with time, and any religious toleration was gradually erased by the Counter Reformation. Nonetheless, Poland (similar to other European nations, but unlike Russia) had early institutions, laws and customs limiting royal power. The Italian city-republics, Flanders and Holland also have their history of struggle for freedom and political rights as well as major efforts against political and religious oppression and domination. But the English experience is unique in its form and clarity of purpose. It was the English Parliament and political culture that had and still has worldwide political and cultural impact and produced a working and efficient form of democratic and benevolent government. It affected the political culture of most, if not all, democratic nations.

In England, gradually, power shifted more and more toward the House of Commons and step by step Parliament extended its control over legislation, taxation and executive power, eventuating in a cabinet responsible to Parliament.[38]

The history of England differs from other European history in this major aspect, for the meaningful drama of English history is above all played out in Parliament. "As it has been said," Trevelyan repeats again, "it is not England who made her Parliaments, but the Parliaments that made England." The parliaments were the places of historical backdrop of struggle for individual rights and liberty by way of limiting the power of the crown, of the powerful lords and eventually of the state which, in its ambivalent quality, protected the weaker against the more powerful. In this historical drama, basic political and human rights were defined, legislated and armed with the protective shield of the rule of law and authority of the state. The very modern political and legal meaning of citizenship matured in this House; although bound by tradition, the term the "signifier," "subject," continued.

THE ORIGIN OF THE MODERN MEANING OF CITIZENSHIP

Today citizenship has several meanings. The most general identifies citizenship with membership in a state, the fact that a given state considers an individual born on its territory or from native parents as its citizen; hence, there are citizens of authoritarian as well as of democratic states. However, citizenship in a modern and democratic sense is associated above all with a government under the rule of law, based on the consent of the members of the state, who also have some part, active or passive, in the government of the country. Even if such participation or authority may appear dubious for some critics, citizens in a democratic country approve their government by means of a vote. The multiparty system secures the openness of debate and choices.

Moreover, the legitimacy of power is based on consent of the governed. Citizenship in a democratic state is associated with a code of human and political rights of all members of the state, who own these rights not due to a common ancestry or a myth of a kinship bond, but due to the very fact of their membership in the state.

It is the culture and the territorial principle, the bond of neighborhood above all individual freedoms and common values that are indisputable, in most democratic countries. The basic principles of the territorial nature of citizenship are of Roman, as well as Greek, origin. But, the modern meaning of principles of political, individual and human rights as an essential part of citizenship was adopted early in England and Britain and later in America. Here they moved from just philosophical and theoretical debates to legally protected institutions. Principles and ideas that appeared in England and were discussed for many years, even centuries, became core matters of legal institutions and policies.

The English and British parliaments spelled out basic civic principles of personal and political freedom. The basic strategy for individual freedom and civic liberty was devised here: the limitation of the power of the state.

Paradoxically, however, the authority of the state, of an efficient and vigorous administration, is needed concurrently (1) to protect the individual and enforce laws that secure freedom and welfare, (2) to take the initiative and intervene in times of crisis and (3) to act when public initiative is imperative. The reconciliation of both principles—on one hand, the limitation of power and on the other, vigorous and efficient administration and government intervention as well as supervision and proper balance—is the art of a democratic government.

The major principles that appeared later in the Bill of Rights or in other laws were discussed and fought for on the floor of Parliament. The right to freedom of speech and publication—hence, later the press—was applied at first to debates and speeches in the English House of Commons, to be extended in time as a general principle, to a right of all free men. The first declarations of freedom of speech in the House of Commons, avowed as early as the fifteenth century, were recognized fully in the Bill of Rights of 1689. Freedom of the press made its passage through the House of Commons slowly, and not without resistance, making its debut with the right to publish debates. Freedom from arrest and immunity for members of Parliament were established here.

The right of those subjects to have representation concerning taxation was also firmly declared here. In England an early bill of rights was enacted that reaffirmed the civic rights of the nation and strengthened any humanitarian tendencies by prohibiting cruel and unusual punishment and protecting subjects against arrest and excessive bail.[39] All these principles were debated here, adding the very institutions of democratic and parliamentary government that were later adopted widely all around the world.

The Jews bestowed principles of ethics and religion on humanity; the Greeks added rudiments and fundamental principles of science and ethics. The British, specially the English nation, endowed mankind with the art of efficient as well as humane government and political institutions. They gave to mankind a pragmatic, workable constitution, rooted in civil liberties as well as the philosophers of this unusual political creed (e.g., Locke, Milton, J. S. Mill, Lord Acton and so many others). They inspired political thinkers and writers in France as well as in the American colonies and affected future political directions toward the advance of a civic and democratic republic.

Here, the very content of modern citizenship was reborn—or born—and spelled out clearly and applied in a pragmatic, workable way, although the term "citizen" did not displace the ancient and traditional term "subject," as it did in France. The meaning of "subject" was changing. In England it meant eventually a free and independent citizen, whose actions were determined by the rule of law and whose duties were decided with his consent. To put it into the frame of reference of Ferdinand de Saussure, one of the masters in the field of semantics, the "subject" was the "signifier," an unchanging sound and image of a dynamic and changing "signified" (the meaning and concept)—which from a "subject" changed into modern civic membership in a state—a citizen.

EARLY "SUBJECTS" IN AMERICA

The centuries-old political heritage of England branched out in America finding its own political current, which led to the development of a modern civic state in its historical meaning comparable to ancient Rome. There is however an obvious weakness in our comparison since antiquity differs so much from our times. The Roman Empire was a slave state (and we compare it to twentieth-century America, not to the antebellum period), not a twentieth-century republic legislating equal rights for all. Moreover, the Roman Empire of the second and third centuries, was an unusual alloy of oriental despotism and surviving republican Roman institutions and symbols; found among these elements was citizenship. Hence, in spite of the differences, citizenship, its nature and relevance, offers the challenge of "comparison." It's true that at times comparison might be a defective, even a deceptive, method of analogy. But in the United States, due to its historical development as a large, almost continental nation of immigrants, citizenship became—not unlike Rome—the political bond of a multiethnic civic state.

The American colonists brought British political culture, traditions and philosophy with them. America was more often than not called a "young country." American political traditions were not new, nor "young"—the roots of American institutions are ancient. Paul Miliukov, a prominent Russian statesman and historian, commented on old and young nations during the dramatic year 1905, when coming revolutions could be sensed and when nascent parliamentary ways began appearing in the Russian Duma. "Nations may be very old in their existence but very young in their civilization." Hence, Russia, continued Miliukov, is an old nation in terms of its material existence, but young in its civilization. America however, of a young "material existence," was a very old civilization in terms of its institutions and political culture.

Both nations (Russia and the United States) were formed as a result of long migrations in foreign territories, among "primitive peoples" (to use Miliukov's nineteenth-century perception). "The American settlers" he continued "brought from their old homes the principles and habits of political liberty and social order. . . . Russian pioneers, on the other hand, began their process when they emerged into history. That's why 'young America's' torch of liberty illuminates the world, while today's 'young Russia' hesitates in a stage equally distant from the modern order and medieval violence unbridled by law."[40]

The colonists of New England brought with them their old political creed and philosophy, which originated in their mother country. They reinterpreted British law and traditions in their own way. The conditions of a new and vast country were quite different than those in England. In addition, the impact of the then advanced British political philosophy was strong indeed. The fact that Locke wrote the Constitution of Carolina was a clear indication of his powerful influence. European Enlightenment and classic traditions shaped the nature of the emerging independent state.

By the seventeenth century a clear distinction was made between "aliens" and "subjects"; furthermore, the law made a distinction between natural born subjects, naturalized subjects and "denizens," legally admitted foreigners. In spite of substantial differences, all may have lived in the same neighborhood and belonged to the same community.[41]

ALLEGIANCE AND LEGITIMACY

At this point we will return for a while to our initial distinction of major original bonds and types and types of states. Medieval and sixteenth-century England, later Britain, was neither a tribal nor a civic state. As in other states in medieval Europe the king, the dynasty, the crown were symbols of unity, loyalty and allegiance. The king or the queen, the dynasty, was the source of allegiance and legitimacy. In this sense it was a dynastic state. The realm was a kind of royal property or at least a reflection of this institution. Subjects owed their allegiance to the crown. This theory of allegiance and subjectship was interpreted in Sir Edward Coke's opinion concerning the *Calvin* case (1608) and Coke's opinion, according to Kettner, "dominated English law for several centuries."[42]

The case was concerned a dispute over a land title, but it was also a test case between the nature of the union between Scotland and England, in consequence of the legal nature of subjectship. In essence, this decision interpreted subjectship as a personal relationship between the subject and the king, a relationship that was part of nature, like the relationship between child and father, a part of the natural order and hierarchy of things.

In addition to subjectship by birth there were many other kinds of allegiance, for example *Ligantia acquisita* (acquired allegiance), by way of conquest, denization or naturalization. Furthermore, *Ligantia* derived from a formal oath of allegiance. All varieties were considered as part of the natural order. Once acquired, as if natural, it established a permanent relationship forever, "a lasting obedience to his natural superior, to the king." This was not a contractual relationship between an individual and the king. It was a part of a "natural order"; being a subject was forever. Whatever the varieties of subjectship, it was a reflection of a permanent, unchanging hierarchical order.[43] Hence, the allegiance was a personal relationship between the king and the subject, not between the individual and his country or individual and his state or *his* nation or *his* city—the Roman *Senatus Populusquae Romanus*—SPQR.

Historically, this type of concept was a consequence and an outgrowth of an original tribal nature of early complex kinship associations of extended families, grouped into clans, where related clans bonded together into tribes and tribes were tied together by memories of common tradition, ancestry and culture. It was ruled by the founder's descendants or mythical memories of the latter. This type of social myth, of a "natural" kinship organization, was associated with the nature of early property.

In cases of the state, which originated by conquest, legitimacy was derived either from religious beliefs, from the sacral nature of the ruler, and/or the rights of the conqueror (his sovereignty over the conquered land and victims was akin to sentiments of property). In fact, "conquest" is an armed robbery, the theft of land in quest of legitimacy so as to secure permanence. The dynastic bond, as long as it was tied to a dominant ruling nationality, had the quality of a "natural" hierarchical order of subordination to the early founding family.

This dynastic bond was a source of legitimacy of incorporation of new territories and peoples into the realm acquired by conquest or by inheritance. In fact, this was also a kind of a broader bond, rooted in a social myth, which tied together diverse people within a single state.

All these relationships of domination and subjectship of inhabitants were wrapped into a solemn rationalization of power, social mythology and general mystique. Some thoughtful persons may have asked an obvious question during the course of human history: why does this man or woman (sometimes a cruel one) reign or rule over the realm and not someone else, better fitted for this position?

Now, we we shall continue with the hierarchical relationship between the subject and the sovereign, the "natural one," as one "between the child and the father." This relationship, even in medieval times, was considered not one sided. True, a subject owned allegiance as a "child does in a family." But the king in turn extended his protection over his subjects. Relationships between the sovereign and subjects also involved mutual duties and rights between the superior and inferior. Such an interpretation, involving hierarchical reciprocity between "superior" and "inferior," the lord and his subjects, contrasted with seventeenth-century theories of natural law and social contract, with the political philosophy of Locke, as well as others, shared by many in the American colonies.

In terms of natural law, this relationship—one between the subject and the ruler as well as the state—was volitional and contractual. In terms of natural law it was an act of human will, a contract that could be also dissolved. Coke interpreted allegiance as a "double and reciprocal bond"—but still, it was not contractual, based on the consent and will of equals, but organized in a "natural" hierarchical relationship between ruler and subjects.

Moreover, in a far off continent, with its immense distance from the center of royal power, such theory was by no means convincing, lacked vigor and the support of the usual visible symbols of power. It was not convincing in terms of the intellectual currents of the time. While in the middle of the seventeenth century, English legal discussions concerned with naturalization stressed that the allegiance of naturalized subjects was personal and perpetual, the colonial approach moved in reverse considering naturalization as volitional and contractual.[44]

THE ROAD TO DEMOCRATIC CITIZENSHIP: CONTRACT VERSUS HIERARCHY

Hence, the bond between the "subject" and the community was more and more considered as a consequence of individual will and decision. Since a contract could be dissolved, subjectship was neither necessarily eternal, nor was it tied to the dominant ethnicity. It was an individual act.

In the American colonies the contractual and consensual interpretation advanced with the new and influential political theories of Enlightenment.[45] It was this general tendency that led to separation of the American concept of subjectship, and later citizenship, from its original British origins. In a slow process of growth, this new and original concept of citizenship developed, which recognized this contractual nature, where a naturalized person exercised his rights of citizenship as well as of termination—if he so wished (unlike the British concept and early tradition).

The situation here was of course quite different from the situation in England. American colonies were communities of immigrants, often of different religions and different nationalities. The circumstances of naturalization in the colonies was much more relevant and wide-ranging than in England. The extended formal procedures practiced in the mother country were difficult to meet in a distant colony. This also contributed to the shifting of naturalization to the local colonial authorities and simplification of the procedures. With this shift to local authorities, the relationship between the immigrant who applied for naturalization and the colony became a matter of relationship between the immigrant and the community and less a case of political connection with a distant metropolitan state and simple subordination to the king.

This change and simplification of naturalization appears early in the fundamental Constitution of Carolina, written by John Locke in 1669, which required only simple formalities. The applicants were asked to sign the constitution and promise their loyalty to the colonial authority. Quite early, William Penn suggested that the newcomers were to be given their rights by a simple act of local assembly. Eventually, the process of naturalization in the American colonies was simplified by Parliament in 1740: Seven years of residence were required as well as an oath before a colonial judge, Jews and Quakers were included; however, naturalization was not yet extended to Catholics.

This shift of naturalization from the metropolis to particular colonies also had its historical impact after the Declaration of Independence. The question arose as to whether citizenship was associated with the state or the nation—whether citizenship was a state or a federal matter. On one hand, the states made their own laws concerning naturalization and citizenship (Rhode Island, Georgia, New Hampshire); on the other hand, Congress had approved a naturalization law in 1795, increasing the period of residence from two to five years and requiring a declaration of intent. This ambiguous and confusing issue of state and federal citizenship continued until the Civil War. It was finally resolved with the Fourteenth and Fifteenth Amendments, ratified respectively in 1868 and 1870, which stated clearly that "all persons born or naturalized in the United States are citizens of United States and the State wherein they reside." The state could not legislate in matters of citizenship.[46]

The very nature of American citizenship in its present meaning came to full fruition in the late 1860s, after the Civil War, with the Thirteenth, Fourteenth and Fifteenth Amendments and the Civil Rights Bill. American citizenship was tied to the federalist nature of government and civil and political rights. Federalism implies a certain diarchy, dualism in distribution of the authority, even sovereignty. Hence, the existence of two centers of power became an issue over whether naturalization and citizenship belonged to the state or to the Union.

A NATIONAL U.S. CITIZENSHIP

American democracy was deeply rooted in local government as well as states' rights, freedom of interference from the central government. During the nineteenth century both sentiments and political practice were far more strongly associated with the state—state patriotism—than today. Some of the states continued to practice discrimination in exercise of elementary civil and political rights. State authorities denied those newly acquired rights: the Thirteenth Amendment of 1865 abolished slavery, the Fourteenth Amendment of 1866–68 decisively "nationalized" citizenship.

National citizenship implied state citizenship, but the supreme authority rested of course with the Union. The development of citizenship was also closely tied to the history of civil and political rights. The United States, the national government, now protected civil rights. The Fifteenth Amendment of 1870 extended federal authority over political rights and protected the right to vote. In those critical years—as Belz put it—nationalization of civil rights took place and "the national government could protect these rights against the state government."[47]

The historical dualism in matters of civil and political rights and citizenship came to an end. Finally, in the Fifteenth Amendment, ratified in 1870, this issue was fully resolved. In the words of the Fifteenth Amendment: the rights of citizens to vote "shall not be denied or abridged" by the federal government or any state "on account of race, color, or previous condition of servitude."

Prior to emancipation and constitutional amendments this duality concerning the concept and nature of citizenship (state versus national) was not only of academic relevance. When slavery was abolished in the New England states, they were among the earliest to abolish this ancient and cruel institution. In Vermont slavery was abolished in 1777, Rhode Island in 1776 (since 1777 African Americans could vote in Rhode Island), Connecticut in 1784, and New York began a gradual process in 1799. By the middle of the nineteenth century, American was divided into free and slave states, and the nature of the citizenship had its impact on the status of African Americans who acquired freedom. This matter was adjudicated in the infamous case of *Dred Scott v. Sanford* (1851) in which an African American from Missouri sued for the freedom he had acquired in Illinois.[48] The Fourteenth Amendment, finally established national citizenship and resolved the problem of duality.

But it took almost a century before the issue of equal rights for black Americans was fully and legally set forth by the Supreme Court. In spite of the Fourteenth Amendment, discrimination, especially segregation, was practiced in many states. The historical decision of 1896 (*Plessy v. Ferguson*), which mandated "separate but equal accommodations for white and colored citizens," legalized the practice of segregation, particularly segregated education. As a rule public education for black Americans was inferior; moreover, segregation was not only humiliating but affected social attitudes and economic opportunities.

In 1954 the Supreme Court in an another historic decision (*Brown v. Board of Education of Topeka*), declared unconstitutional the segregation of Negro students in the public schools. The court declared that the "separate but equal" doctrine denied equal educational opportunity to all children and was inherently unequal, ordering at the same time deseg-regation. This decision prompted sweeping movements toward deseg-regation and racial equality, spearheaded by federal authorities and civil rights movements, culminating under President Lyndon Johnson's administration in the Civil Rights Act (1964–65)—a legal turning point for this historic trend toward racial equality.

African Americans have seen great advancement since the 1960s, and while prejudice continues in various degrees, overt discrimination has substantially declined, especially in areas of public policy. In many cases legal discrimination has been reversed, affected by strong federal policies (such as Affirmative Action), which insured preferential treatment for ethnic and racial minorities. The legal duality as well as the dual status of citizen—relative to race—which was different for whites and different for African Americans—ended. The concept of citizenship was now firmly identified with individual, human and political rights and the protection of all native born and naturalized citizens.

The civic state today means a state in which citizenship is not only a political bond of members of the state, but also a state that secures effective civil rights—broadly conceived—for all citizens, a state that does not practice any form of racial, ethnic or religious discrimination.

Individual or group prejudice cannot be eliminated by a single decision, by a single law. To diminish prejudice calls for a long process of education and change. But discrimination practiced by a government is a different matter. Once discrimination had been put effectively outside the law, and authorities ceased to apply policies of discrimination, the civic state in its full meaning came into being.

THE ROAD TOWARD ETHNIC PLURALISM

The history of American citizenship is one of a changing institution, from an exclusive racial to an all-inclusive civic association. It is here, that the model of a contemporary advanced citizenship in a multiethnic state has been created. It is a device of association of free men and women. Admission to the membership in a state is not an act of submission to a higher hierarchy. It is an agreement between a new member and a state, a contract of mutual obligations, a concept close to the eighteenth-century idea of social contract. It is a device which is well designed for a union of peoples of different origin, religion, culture, ethnicity or of race. They all are citizens. Hence, it is a fitting model for a multiethnic or multicultural state, a pluralistic one where diversity is accepted and unity is paramount.

Thus, American citizenship departed from its colonial model of "subjectship," when it became a concept of consensual relationship between an individual and the state, a doctrine of a free person, distant from the early hierarchical theory. The American doctrine advanced toward a contractual and consent doctrine, a doctrine of a free individual who, in the case of naturalization, acquired citizenship in return for duties and loyalty, as a consequence of his personal choice and consent. Hence Congress declared (July 27, 1868): "The right of repatriation is a natural and inherent right of all people." A native can relinquish his birthright, a naturalized person may repatriate by his own choice and decision. However, the British tradition continued, in the very meaning of the political content of citizenship as well as in continuation of the formal procedure within the American judicial system.

With the rise of nationalism, European citizenship in many countries had been fused with ethnic identity even with the mystique of a single common ancestry, while American citizenship, especially in the second half of the twentieth century, became more and more inclusive and removed from its earlier provisions, its racial and ethnic barriers that narrowed its universal quality. Europeans, in the nineteenth century and early part of the twentieth century, because of nationalism, often followed a more narrow concept, closely attached to ethnic origin.

This is changing today, especially in Western Europe, and a broader interpretation is accepted, resulting in legislation that helps absorb large sections of the immigrant population. Nevertheless, in Europe this problem is far more difficult to resolve since Europe is not a traditional continent of immigrants, and the large influx of new immigrants is a rather recent phenomenon and different in nature from the past.

Our theme however is not one of jurisprudence and legal interpretation. Citizenship is far more than a dry, legal letter. The changing content of the concept is a reflection of changes in cultural political philosophy—in the general ideology of a multiethnic state, it corresponds to profound changes in the nature of our society and in our approach to problem solving. The symbol of citizenship has its historical and political content, a sociological meaning. The nature of a multiethnic state is expressed in this institution. Legal aspects however affect only part of this wide spectrum of social and political ideas and relationships.

Today, the dominant public policy, strongly reflected in American daily life, is a policy of cultural and ethnic pluralism, which is rather a recent development. Contemporary pluralistic policies have their philosophical roots in the very beginnings of the Republic, as evidenced by the separation of church and state. The political identity of the citizen is now clearly separated from ethnicity, race or religion. The United States, a nation of immigrants of diverse nationalities, was of course different in its origin and nature than the European or non-European tribal or national states. Still, prejudice toward newcomers was often strong to begin with (e.g., Irish Catholics of the nineteenth century, as well as with the Eastern and Southern European mass migration at the turn of the century and later).

Citizenship acquired the specific and distinctive meaning of an institution of fundamental significance, respected and desired by most immigrants, not unlike the ancient Roman citizenship that was longed for by Latin allies. It was indeed far more than material advantages that citizenship offered to newcomers. Citizenship is and it was part of America's successful and attractive experiment and associated with political tradition and other institutions of the Republic. In 1880 when Henry Schliemann, the discoverer of Troy, published his major work on Mycenae, the German American archaeologist and author identified himself on the title page of his classic volume by citing: "by Dr. Henry Schliemann, citizen of the United States of America, author of *Troy and Its Remains*." Schliemann expressed his sentiments in this simple but telling way as he attained worldwide recognition.

For immigrants from Eastern or Southern Europe, from Russia or Italy, and particularly for those of peasant or working class origins, citizenship also meant, more often than not, a social and economic advance. They benefited from a more secure and dignified social and political status in their relations with American authorities, a respected status they did not enjoy in the Old Country, where class divisions were far deeper and sanctified by history and tradition. Although the fathers of the Republic were of British origin, from its earliest times citizenship and political identity were not as strongly tied to a single ethnicity as was the case in Europe.

Changes in immigration laws, particularly in the last four decades, resulted in substantial immigration from Asia, the Caribbean and Latin America. At the same time, illegal immigration increased, especially to the southwestern states. While the ethnic mix was changing and becoming even more diversified than in the past, citizenship and civic identification became an even more fundamental bond in integrating the variety of diverse ethnic communities, which differed in culture far more than during early European immigration.

Sometimes, in moments of crisis, small but vocal and militant parties of ethnic or racial minority groups propagate their own narrow and antagonistic kind of nationalism and separatism hidden behind misused symbols and a shield of multiculturalism. In such situations a civic bond—which claims not only rights but stresses also the allegiance, duties and responsibilities of a citizen—becomes essential as a condition of unity and national solidarity.

The present nature of American citizenship, and ethnic as well as racial policies, is the fruit of a long historical developmental change. Political and cultural attitudes have changed too. During the nineteenth century and later, prejudices against and discrimination of the hard-working immigrant were very strong in many sections of the native population. In spite of those prejudices, a historical trend toward acceptance and integration of the immigrant into the American community prevailed in our times, but it was a tendency expressed through legislation, judicial decisions and public policies, slowly evolving toward an inclusive civic state. It was a historical process, but the tendency was there at the beginning, a tendency strong enough to advance toward the present kind of civic state.

THE MEANING OF THE TERM DEMOCRATIC CITIZENSHIP

Today, the term "citizen" is in general use. It appears in the constitutions of democratic states as well as in the laws of totalitarian states. For purposes of this book, our major interest is of course in the citizenship of a democratic nature, associated with the consent of the governed, respect for political and human rights and some participation in public affairs. But, the term is indiscriminately used and the content varies.

Nevertheless, the two fundamental principles of the original social bond—kinship, tribe and ethnicity on one hand, and neighborhood-territorial principles on the other hand, also appear in a country's laws concerning the civic family as *jus sanguinis* (citizenship based on "blood kinship") and *jus soli* or *loci* (citizenship rooted in "soil," place, territory), where a person was born. Furthermore, the definition of citizenship calls for a distinction between legal, ideological, philosophical and sociological concepts. The legal definition of citizenship, of course, is defined by the laws of a particular country.

A political party may advance an ideological concept of citizenship, and this concept may vary with the political orientations of other social movements. The nationalist right advances an ideological definition of citizenship—which is exclusive and differs from the one advocated by liberals.

The social-philosophical concepts of citizenship within the civic family may vary too. They reflect views on rights and duties of an individual as a member of a state, as well as the philosophical and abstract premises of the concept, not necessarily related to the empirical reality of "what is," but also postulating "what ought to be."

Furthermore, the sociological approach to citizenship primarily concerns the social-empirical realities, data, relationships and actions, that actually take place and affect society and the culture of a nation. It is difficult to separate the three approaches, especially an action-oriented ideology from a pragmatic but still visionary philosophy. Moreover, ideology and philosophy, directly or indirectly, by means of votes, affect legislation and may also influence judicial decisions.

General political perceptions and philosophies also affect concepts and interpretations, as well as applications. Conservatives prefer to limit the power of the state and extend the private sphere of activities of the independent civil society rather than approve state-controlled actions administered by bureaucracies. The emphasis is on the individual, his freedom of action and on limitation of the power and intervention of the state. Liberals, in an American definition of this term, are prone to extend state intervention and support social legislation that enhances the very concept of the rights of a citizen by setting limits and restricting an individual's freedom in his economic relations that in an unrestricted free market economy is guided by profit only, not by public interest.

Changing political, demographic, economic and social conditions affect policies and attitudes toward acceptance of foreign-born inhabitants and inhabitants of foreign ancestry into the fold of citizenry. This is again a sociological problem. The very concept and application of the institution of citizenship has both inclusive and exclusive functions—it excludes from or limits opportunities and rights for those who do not qualify as citizens but who inhabit a common territory.

Hence, the legal definition of citizenship changes with changing legislation, which in turn is affected by dynamic social and demographic processes. Ideological concepts and projects related to citizenship also change, and here programs and concepts vary along ideological lines. Since situations may vary in different countries, so do definitions. Nonetheless, a general philosophy of citizenship and of the civil nature of a democratic state, the "essentials," are common to all democratic and—let us not hesitate to add—in civilized states (even if some provision or interpretation of the principles of human and political rights, or of territorial, political identity may vary). It is also a matter of degree.

THE NATIONAL CULTURE AND CITIZENSHIP

The dominant connection between national culture, between the culture of the original, the "core" or "root" nation, and the state continues even in the most liberal civic states, which promote actively the principle of separation of political identity and rights from ethnicity by such radical means as a rigorous application of affirmative action with no limits on its duration. After all, the civic state has been created and exists due to the "core nation." The American civic state has been the fruit of American history, American culture, and more specific its political culture.

In terms of theory, we may consider the civic state as a state of complete separation of ethnic and cultural bond and identity from the political state. This is however an abstract, "ideal" model, not an empirical one, and perhaps not the best one. Civic institutions, which grew and were tested by historical experience, became a part of constitutional and legal systems of other democratic and national states. It was easier to apply the civic principle of relative separation of ethnicity from the political bond in those states that historically were both originated and advanced by immigrants (e.g., the United States or other American states, where immigrants were needed to develop the country). Here, an additional political bond, a broader political one, rooted in the traditions and institutions of the dominant nationality—a political bond of all members of the state, irrespective of their origin—suggested a workable, pragmatic answer to problems of nationality and to the integration of culturally and linguistically diverse groups.

In those polities, the state demanded from a citizen a civic loyalty but included the foreign born or person of foreign ancestry into the community. He enjoyed all citizen rights and protection in exchange for his willingness to reciprocate with his civic duties and responsibilities. His ethnic or religious affiliation or identity was of no political concern, save those cases when they infringed on laws or rights of others.

But the very existence of a massive immigrant population does not per se favor a civic state. The humane and civic ways of integrating the immigrant population are a consequence of the basic, initial political culture of the host state. Wealthy Arab Gulf states have a large immigration of workers from Asian countries, but the states and governments are exclusive and discriminating, especially when the religion of the immigrants differs from the host nation.

Whatever criticisms and reservations we may have, the United States, in the last decades of this century, created its own model of a civic state, which was rooted in civil rights and cultural pluralism under the rule of law. In spite of adversity, it was rather an unusual historical case of a large, continental state, composed of huge varieties of cultures, religions, races and political and cultural tendencies, that worked well and efficiently to provide stability and create conditions of prosperity for large sections of inhabitants as well as respect for the political and human rights of all. Massive illegal immigration from such distant lands as China, and as close as Haiti or Cuba, illegal immigration under threatening conditions of insecure transport through perilous waters, is evidence of the image and hope this country displays.

TWO MAJOR PATTERNS: FRANCE AND GERMANY

With the variety of cultures and histories worldwide, it is hardly possible or advisable to apply the same constitutional system to all diverse nation-states. The problem is how to apply basic civic concepts and notions to different constitutional and political systems. During the declining years of our century Western European countries, Latin America, Canada, Australia, New Zealand, India and other states have done it in a variety of ways, and in varying degrees. It is however beyond the scope of this book to present an extensive study of these dissimilar laws and philosophies of citizenship. We shall limit our discussion to brief comments and to two representative examples—of France and Germany—both national states and members of a broad civic family.

Modern nations, while practicing civic principles, followed two major patterns: citizenship acquired by birth from citizen parents (*jus sanguinis*, "by blood," common descent) and citizenship acquired by birth on national territory (*jus soli* or *jus loci*, law based on the territorial principle).

This all goes back to the basic and ancient principles of kinship and neighborhood: citizenship acquired by birth of parents who belong to dominant ethnicity or nationality (the "core-nation," a common-descent principle) or acquired by birth on the national territory (the territorial or neighborhood principle). These two principles have (and also had) wide application in policies of naturalization. The territorial principle facilitates separation of the political membership of a person in the state from ethnicity and creates a new, second bond—the civic bond. Thus, it is the device of dual identity, the "principle" of common descent, which makes such separation difficult, if possible at all.

In various national legislations, these two principles are applied in a variety of ways. This is important in processes of naturalization, vital for immigrant populations. The European practice of both principles was also applied in a complementary way with various degrees of exclusion or inclusion. The common descent principle of "common blood" is associated with and derived from the earlier forms of a tribal state. The territorial principle (*jus soli*) has been widely applied in the United States and in ancient Rome. In Rome it was eventually codified during imperial times (see chapter 2).

Germany continued with the principle of common descent—with the consanguinal principle—but still, the new, democratic nation-state extended basic human rights to all legally admitted inhabitants.

The two opposite principles show up clearly in the legal and political history and practice of France and Germany. The different historical origins of the ideology of nationhood in France and Germany, their different political and cultural development, affected the basic concept and institution of citizenship. We owe thanks to Brubaker's comprehensive and illuminating comparative study and insight on citizenship and nationhood, which gives us a better understanding of those variations.[49]

The French Revolution could be considered the impetus to the early rise of modern nationalism. France however at that time was a divided nation; it is difficult to speak about a single unitary nation. It was deeply divided into regional-cultural and local groups, in a sense ethnic cultures, and there were also substantial differences in language, history and local traditions.

Moreover, France was separated socially by a legal system that was different for different estates, including major privileges for some. The unitary state—the concept of single nation—was imposed "from above" by political means, by centralizing policies of the state. The unitary state was in a sense imposed on a conglomerate of diverse and disparate French provinces. These centralizing tendencies had already appeared of course under the monarchy. But the institutions of the revolution, as de Tocqueville commented, originated in the preceding period of the "Old Regime" and matured during the revolution.[50]

During the early French Republic the concepts concerning the nation and citizenship were territorial and political, not ethnic nor racial. Such were the views expressed by some leading members of the French National Convention. To quote Brubaker, Siéyès defined the nation as "a body of associates living under common law and represented by the same legislatures." Talien, another prominent member of the convention, commented in 1795: "The only foreigners in France are the bad citizens." This meant that every inhabitant who supported the laws and philosophy of the republic was a citizen.

The core principle of the French Revolution was liberty. The French Constitution of 1791 extended the rights of men to all inhabitants. Nonetheless, French nationalism appeared rather early. The idea of a "nation" gained in appeal during the revolution and ensuing wars and in France's early imperial times. Nevertheless the concept of the nation was not racial, not even ethnic. The political-territorial principle was well established and the concept of nationality was understood as political identity, identity with the French Republic, the French state.

Napoleon supported this definition of nationality, a principle that of course was also favorable to the needs of a large conscript army, since the territorial principle was more inclusive than the ethnic one. But during a later stage, French nationalism also affected the French Revolution. The Jacobins were xenophobic, "anti-foreign."

In spite of the vicissitudes of ideas, the general territorial tendency persisted, and the citizenship laws of 1889, basic to the republic, applied also to the territorial principle. "The French citizenship," wrote Brubaker, "was markedly open to immigrants." Legal citizenship was defined by a combination of both principles: birth and domicile. The 1889 legislation was basic for French citizenship and although it had major revisions, France extended citizenship to most persons born on its territory.[51]

The political-territorial principle was (and is) however integrated in France with cultural-national assimilation. It was not an American type of "multicultural" pluralism, although in daily practice, as far as human and political rights were concerned, there was little difference with the application of a broad pluralistic principle by a moderate or liberal public administration. (True, Chinatown, New York, has Chinese street signs and a Chinese telephone book, and in banks not only Spanish but

also Chinese appears in automatic banking.) Nonetheless, today a foreigner in France enjoys basic rights; France is after all one of the models
of a civilized state and society.

Citizenship is both exclusive and inclusive. It is exclusive to outsiders,
visitors, or foreign-born residents. Today "exclusive" usually means limitations concerning the rights of permanent domicile, exclusion from political rights, as well as limitation of economic opportunities and
exclusion from many social services and benefits of a modern democratic
citizenship.

French citizenship is more inclusive than German citizenship. Nonetheless, Germany offers a host of social benefits, and German legislation
was generous toward those seeking asylum, as well as toward exiles and
guest workers. But the immigrant worker, a noncitizen, as a rule, has a
lower status and is subject to some limitations. In general, the tendency
of a territorial principle is more inclusive toward all inhabitants born on
the territory of the state, which is proper and suitable in a multiethnic
state.

In contrast, the German definition of citizenship, rooted in the principle of common ethnicity—understood often as a community of common culture and tradition rather than of the same tribal origin, while in
the not so distant past "race" was the essential concept—had a rather
exclusive tendency.

The past dictates the present. The difference between those two definitions is of course a result of a different history, of a long development
of ideas and philosophies, which shaped attitudes and political views
and at the end were articulated with different definitions, at first ideological and later legal. "The overall rate of civic incorporation for immigrants," writes Brubaker, "is ten times higher in France than in
Germany."

While 1.5 million Turks residing in Germany (among them 400,000
who were German born) are not citizens, ethnic German immigrants
from the Soviet Union, Poland and other countries (over a million in
1988–1991) received automatic full citizenship as a consequence of different political philosophy and policies.[52]

Since the end of Nazism, German policies toward foreign-born residents have been liberal and understanding, even generous. Still a traditional view prevails, that is: Germany is not an immigration state,
comparable to the United States, or even France, which also has a long
although different tradition of immigration. By 1992, in Germany, 6.5
million out of a total population of about 82 million were foreign nationals. As Kuechler argues, whatever the name, Germany has to consider the fact that a large section of inhabitants are of different, at times
non-European culture, that it is at present an immigrant nation.[53]

The laws of naturalization are more restrictive in Germany than in

France. This consequence of a different historical development appears not only in political views but also in hard facts. The German concept of a nation shared by many is organic; it is a closely knit ethnic community that in the past identified with a single race.

The French concept of nationality, which affected policies and law, is closely associated with the idea of a unitary French state as well as a community of culture, whatever the origin of the inhabitants. Within the nation-states, however, there are differing views as to who should be included as a citizen. Ideologically and philosophically there is not of course a single definition shared by all as to who should be considered a national and included as a citizen. These differences in views appear in numerous German opinion polls.[54]

In spite of all these differences, both in France and Germany, foreigners enjoy a wide range of social assistance protection. The situation may be changing, due to vast numbers of foreign nationals and the pressure of nationalist political parties. Nevertheless, in spite of differences in definition, the civic principle, *sensu largo*—as a recognition of individual rights—is respected by both states. Moreover, the rise of the European Community has also affected the very concept of nationality; a citizen of the European Community enjoys special status.

Again, this is not just an issue of dry legal principles. The laws can be written (the paper is patient). The issue concerns daily life and how legislation is applied and policies enforced. The civic policies in a multiethnic state, like the United States and also Europe, are tested everyday in schools, businesses, the armed forces as well as other aspects of daily life (in the banks, streetcars and eating places). Here is the test, in the social "landscape" of daily activities.

But, it should not be forgotten that the effectiveness of even the most generous legislation and policy does not depend solely on the majority of the "root nation" or the state. Attitudes, values, the behavior of ethnic or cultural minorities and actions of minority groups are a seminal factor in the success or failure of civic democratic policies.

CITIZENSHIP AND SOCIAL RIGHTS

Modern citizenship was not limited solely to its ancient civic and political roots. During the nineteenth century, the state had assumed various measures and responsibilities in the areas of social and economic welfare as well as the health of its citizens. During the eighteenth century, during the Enlightenment, the state had assumed responsibilities in the field of education. Since that time, the rights of citizens have been extended to include a wide area of legal protection and social assistance.

The growth of this tendency culminated, in the midst of the twentieth century, in the emergence of the welfare state—the very concept of citizenship, its definition, being further modified. New social rights had been granted and this extended once again the authority of the government, hence the state, into the social sphere, for example, the introduction of minimum wages, social security, and general labor legislation.

In the American, pluralistic, civic state, the ideological and philosophical definition of citizenship was also affected by this trend. The United States had its own tradition and social practice, its own social-philanthropic infrastructure, different from the European model. But labor legislation was far less advanced than in Europe and the general approach to social change and basic reform was different.

Next to this general, rather individualistic tradition, which continues, the influence of an aggressive social Darwinism in business did not disappear either. In times of early capitalism, wages and work conditions were dictated primarily by unrestrained market forces, driven by profit and deprived of ethical consideration or moderation. Views and policies have changed since those times, but some of these tendencies still pervade some industries where there is opposition to any regulation or limits to the pursuit of higher gains.

On the other hand, philosophical and ideological trends, social and political movements and a powerful labor movement, well organized and often aggressively led, had its impact on the general outlook about the rights of the working man and responsibilities of the state. Those views differed fundamentally from nineteenth-century theories and views of social Darwinism that were influential in social science teaching in American universities at the turn of the century and were also a dominant philosophy of business.

Today the social component of citizenship appears clearly in its modern definition; it is an extended and broad perception of citizenship. It is defined in such terms by scholars, who, to cite Bendix and Marshall, define citizenship in terms of three types of rights—individual (such as liberty of a person, freedom of speech, thought, right of property), political (the franchise, access to public office) and social (the right to economic welfare and security).[55]

These rights are not just declaratory statements (at least not in advanced and democratic industrial nations); they are really applied and enforced. They are also clearly defined in laws, in constitutions, not solely in European or Western legislation. Hence, the 1980 constitution of India (which is quite bulky, over 230 pages, compared to the seven articles of the U.S. Constitution), stipulates in Article 41 the right to work, education and public assistance.

Furthermore, Article 43 commits the state to a "living wage for workers," and spells out the details of suitable legislation. There is of course also in this case a difference between declaration and reality. Can the government of India honor these broad commitments? But the very statement of these rights, in the case of India, is indicative of times, intentions and needs.

Eighteenth-century constitutions, during the age of Enlightenment, did not contain any of these rights. Neither the U.S. Bill of Rights nor the French Declaration of the Rights of Man and Citizen contain definitions or commitments relating to work, employment, or broad protective rights for working people. The new industrial era was at its very beginnings of course. But also social-political philosophy was different.

Formulation of social rights of citizens appears also in contemporary international treaties. Thus, the Maastrich Treaty signed in February 1992, the historical document that establishes the European Union as well as common citizenship, spells out the rights of citizens as well as social policies. A "Protocol" that reaffirms the Social Charter of 1989 also contains an Agreement on Social Policy of the eleven member states that signed the charter and concerns the implementation of the latter.

The legal definition, the actual words of the constitution, does not at all mean that the letter of the law had been translated actually into active policies and implemented by working institutions. The words of law may be empty declarations. The Stalinist constitution of the Soviet Union, as well as constitutions of other communist states had long sections on the political and individual rights of citizens, but these were never applied.

In many countries, social legislation was fully implemented and welfare states were established to assist citizens in employment, enforce protective labor laws and administer health services to an extent unknown in the past history of mankind. At the same time, in democratic states, political and individual rights of citizens were fully respected.

The social rights of citizens form an important tie with the state, not with the ethnic group; hence, their significance in building or reinforcing a multiethnic civic state, or civic elements in a national state. The entire field of social legislation, which extends substantial benefits to citizens, creates a vital, personal link and interest, a "social contract" with the state.

These interests bind the entire multiethnic community and call for attention, action, and, at times, common defense of the acquired rights of all—irrespective of ethnicity or religion. In consequence, they reinforce the civic bond and encourage solidarity in this area for all citizens, not just for those of common ethnic origin or religion.[56]

The vital role of the state in the social arena of course extends the powers of the state. This is considered by many conservatives as an unwanted development or direction. However, to transfer part of this vast area to voluntary associations or civil society is neither feasible nor practical.

All this is an extension of citizens' rights and takes the definition of citizenship beyond the historical and traditional concepts of antiquity or Enlightenment. They are the consequence of a fundamental social and economic change—from an ancient or feudal form of economy to one of an industrial and postindustrial society.

This trend toward the extension of the modern state and major functions of government already appeared by the end of the eighteenth century. There were two major changes that prompted this development. The fundamental one was the Industrial Revolution. With the advent of the modern factory system and influx of working men into the cities, coal mines and later industrial centers, new social problems appeared in Western society, among them unemployment, both seasonal and structural. The second was an emergence of a powerful labor movement—unions and socialist parties.

Arnold Toynbee (the uncle of the historian A. J. Toynbee), in his Oxford lectures (1880–81) on the Industrial Revolution, attached this term to this historical economic change. His conclusions and warnings are still pertinent today. "The effects of the Industrial Revolution prove that free competition may produce wealth without producing well being. We all know the horrors that ensued in England before it was restrained by legislation and combination."[57]

The workers at that time were entirely unprotected against the hazards of unemployment, sickness or accidents. In feudal times, journeymen, artisans and apprentices belonged to guilds, and guilds secured at least some protection and assistance.

Paradoxically, the movement for individual liberty was associated with legislation directed against freedom of association, hence workers' unions. In France, under the powerful impact of Rousseau's philosophy of social contract and theory of general will, the leaders of the revolution called for the abolition of all intermediary associations, such as guilds, which would impede the expression of a national general will.

Unlike the medieval corporate state, where individuals were represented by an intermediary of their corporations, the philosophy of the eighteenth century advanced the creed of individual liberty and direct relations between individual and the state. "It is a great law of social development that the movement from slavery to freedom is also a movement from security to insecurity of maintenance. There is a close connection between the growth of freedom and growth of pauperism; it is scarcely too much to say that the latter is the price we pay for the former," wrote Toynbee a century ago.[58]

How true his words are even today—although conditions have changed greatly. Philosophy and political creed and of course economic interests impeded formation of unions.

Policies toward a direct relationship between the individual and the state, which Bendix called "a plebicitarian relationship," made their mark in weakening, if not annihilating, workers' efforts to combine in their actions in defense of their vital social and economic interests. During the French Revolution Lois Le Chapelier was directed against the formation of independent associations, and Chapelier himself argued that the general will of the nation should not be impeded by intermediary organizations.

In a speech before the National Assembly in 1791, he argued against any corporate organization that would represent and defend the interests of the workers and again paradoxically for the duty of the state to assist the workers and supply opportunities for employment. The essence of these arguments had far-reaching consequences—it meant the extension of the rights of citizens to social-economic areas, the obligation of the state to provide economic security for its citizens.

Here, in contradictory argument, are—it seems to me—the early if not the first arguments, in favor of what was called later the welfare state. Speaking against workers' association—what we would call today unionization—Chapelier at the same time advanced demands for public intervention and more public works.

> The bodies in question have the avowed object of procuring relief for workers in the same occupation who fall sick or become unemployed. But there be no mistake about this. It is for the nation and for the public officials on its behalf to supply work for those who need it for their livelihood and to succor the sick. . . . It should be not permissible to citizens of certain occupations to meet together in defense of their pretended common interests. There must be no more guilds in the state, but only the individual interest of each citizen and the general interest. No one should be allowed to arouse in any citizen any kind of intermediate interest to separate him from the public weal through the medium of corporate interests.[59]

Here, in contradictory argument, we can see an extension of the meaning of citizenship: the inclusion of social rights. The struggle for freedom of association took several decades before the rights of the workers to form unions and to "combine," to associate in defense of their vital interests, had been fully and legally recognized.

A relatively simple way to provide employment was through public works with such projects as road building, irrigation, regulation of rivers, and so forth. Public works for the state and the rulers had been popular since antiquity. Egypt and Rome were examples of extensive public enterprises—as useless as the pyramids of the Pharaohs and as useful as the aqueducts, roads and bridges built by the Romans or the irrigation systems in the Near East and all over Asia.

But public works prior to industrial times were not a consequence of social policies of full employment of free men. In fact, during ancient times this type of work was often—although not always—done by slaves. Unemployment appeared as a consequence of repetitive and frequent crisis during times of industrialization. The growing labor movement advocated state intervention in securing employment, protection against exploitation, limitation of working time, insurance against accidents at work and sickness—all these demands were part of a program of powerful socialist, social-democratic and trade union movements that grew as a major political force since the middle of the nineteenth century.

Their appeals spoke about the new rights of workers. What this really meant in pragmatic terms, at least for the moderate so-called reformist sections of this powerful movement, was an extension of citizens' rights into a new field of public responsibility vital to solving the social-economic problems of the new industrial times.

On one hand, political parties, which represented the early labor movement, adopted ideologies of total transformation of the society; on the other hand, labor leaders advocated, next to basic changes, pragmatic reforms and labor legislation, state intervention and regulation of labor relations. This meant of course an extension of citizens' rights.

Early radical and uncompromising tendencies, appeared at the end of the eighteenth century with various plans for a perfect society, most of them utopian and abstract in nature. But, in the middle of the nineteenth century, pragmatic and constructive groups also voiced demands for necessary labor legislation and provisions that would secure employment for the growing labor force.

UNFOLDING OF SOCIAL RIGHTS OF CITIZENSHIP

The quest for citizens' rights to work and schemes for full employment appeared before the Revolution of 1848. In his essay, *Organisation du Travail*, Louis Blanc advocated for the responsibility of the state for full employment of citizens and suggested the formation of public workshops (*ateliers public*) that would absorb the unemployed working force. These public workshops, he suggested, would be integrated and covered by mutual insurance in order to cover losses of the less successful enterprises.[60]

During the Revolution of 1848 there were also pressures from "below," from the workers, for demands of full employment. During the early days of the revolution, armed representatives of the workers, sought directly from the Provisional Government the right to work. Louis Blanc, a member of the government, after a talk with the delegation, proposed a decree in which the Provisional Government committed itself to guarantee the workers employment through public work.

Lorenz von Stein, a contemporary historian of social movements, notes that it was incomprehensible, how reasonable men could issue such a decree. Blanc was one of the fathers of so-called state socialism, which had its impact in Europe, especially a generation later in Germany.

The line of thinking was rather simple and convincing: since capitalism resulted in unemployment, the most powerful institution, which in fact controlled the economy—the state—had the responsibility to provide an answer to the social-economic dilemma of its citizens. It was also the state that could prevent the misery of the unemployed. And indeed, on February 26, 1848, a decree was published establishing Blanc's national workshops. His plan was applied by the government but, historians tell us, with no success.[61]

Nonetheless, step by step the rights of citizenship extended into the social-economic area. The Revolution of 1848 was a turning point in redefining major functions of the modern state; consequently there was a redefinition of citizens' rights changing the very concept of citizenship and recognizing social rights.

The Provisional Government introduced a number of reforms. One such reform reduced working time from eleven to ten hours. Although only one hour, this was indeed a substantial change as the working time for various industries in Europe was often as long as twelve, even sixteen hours. Moreover, for the first time, a Ministry of Progress, which in fact was a kind of Department of Labor, had been established, and employment and "right to work" became a major issue.[62]

Von Stein considered the 1848 revolution in France a turning point in the history of the labor movement. This was the time, he argued, when modern social democracy was created. The revolution was indeed a historical time when the functions of the state were extended into the vast social-economic area.

In consequence, the nature of modern state has been redefined and so was the very concept of citizenship. Next to the political and civil rights, social rights have been recognized.

Moreover, the direction of future long-term development was established, in spite of the fact that the experiment in social and political democracy ended with the return of a new Bonapartism. It was, however, the beginning of a political trend that culminated a century later in the establishment of the welfare state, although neither the name nor the form of the future state had been anticipated.

This was the period when powerful mass movements were activated by visions of a perfect utopian society rather than by sober, melioristic but attainable plans and projects. On the other hand, it was also a historical moment of initiation of labor legislation and the beginnings of parliamentary participation for representatives of the working class in constructive, day-by-day legislative work and government.

Since then, in spite of the failure of revolutions and visions of a perfect state, large sections of the working and politically active population considered social problems—above all the protection of labor—a major public function of the government and the state and part of its civic mission.

During the declining decades of the nineteenth century a new development occurred, not a political mass movement but one of intellectual groups, particularly of German university professors, and gained soon the name "socialism of the academic chair," *Katheder Socialismus*. Unlike the social democrats, this group did not advocate a fundamental transformation of the economy, but suggested the extension of state functions to the economic and social areas, stressing the responsibility of the state for the welfare of the working class.

It is beyond the scope of this book to discuss the entire doctrine. Its defenders were oriented toward practical and efficient democratic answers to social and economic problems and they stressed the need for protection of workers against exploitation; they emphasized the role or mission of the state as the paramount public institution responsible for the welfare of its citizens.

A century ago in Germany, Bismarck introduced extensive social legislation such as health and accident insurance for workers. For Bismarck, this was also a political strategy directed against the growing influence and power of the social democrats, whose reformist wing advocated the need for similar reforms. Whatever the reason, Bismarck's policies extended state functions to areas of social problems; he was associated with benefits for the workers, citizens of the German state. In consequence, the very concept of citizenship was redefined again in Germany, as it was in other states; citizenship was now associated with the social rights of its members.

Toward the end of the nineteenth century labor legislation had been greatly advanced in Europe. The interwar period (1918–1939), a quarter century between the two world catastrophes, was indeed the time of unusual bloom for labor and social legislation. The reform movement was now spearheaded by powerful and influential social-democratic parties and trade unions. Most of them—but far from all—were influenced by the theories of Marx and Engels. Marx ignored facts that would weaken his perfectly logical theories and approach; he advanced a rather primitive and negative theory of state, which was only only partly valid.

Marx disregarded advances in social legislation and the nature of state intervention and regulation. Engels had a broader and more practical outlook. He was also more reform oriented and pointed to and appreciated the unusual social progress the working class had made in the latter part of the nineteenth century (e.g., see his preface to his new edition to *The Conditions of the Working Class in England*, [1892]; the first edition was published in 1845).[63]

The entire period from 1789–1939, but particularly 1918–1939, was also a time of plans for and ideas about a perfect state. The utopian visions, however, failed in the great experiments of the twentieth century as well as in local, experimental socialist colonies of the nineteenth century. Not the seekers of a perfect, utopian state, but the melioristic, more practical and moderate reform-oriented socialists, the social-democrats succeeded in the twentieth century.

Working toward the welfare state and the continuous improvement of labor conditions, labor legislation—which extended the social commitments of the state—was a consequence of the ideas, actions and pressures of the reform-oriented and more practical leadership and support initiated by Louis Blanc in France and by Ferdinand Lassalle in Germany. However, in Germany, the advanced social legislation was the result of a long and complex social-historical process that cannot be reduced to a single cause or credited to unique heroes.

The communist parties, supported by the Soviet Union, were above all parties committed to the total utopian transformation of society; they were not just parties of reform. Their ideal was the perfect communist state, as prescribed by Lenin and Stalin, and national parties were subservient to orders from Moscow. But fear of a communist upheaval and the pressure of political opinions also affected the tendency toward accepting reforms and extending protective legislation. For communists offered the alternative of a totalitarian dictatorship, which was not attractive; it was a frightening concept for most of the people.

International conventions formed a safeguard for many protective laws, for example, the number of working hours and the prohibition of employment of children and women in certain industries. The International Labor Organization (ILO), established in Geneva as an agency of the League of Nations, coordinated international activities in this area with conferences, publications and initiatives, and above all international conventions.

Instead of a perfect state of social justice, slowly a new model of a welfare state emerged, a polity that assumed social responsibility.

The United States moved very slowly behind the European reforms. This wealthy and highly industrialized and advanced society had, at that time, only a modicum of social legislation compared to other European nations that were relatively poor and technologically and economically far less advanced. For example, Czechoslovakia and Poland already had well-established universal health insurance systems, advanced labor legislation and effective state intervention in labor relations exercised by special courts or mediation commissions.

The United States entered a new era of progress during the Roosevelt administration. New labor legislation followed American traditions and ways. Unique agreements and institutions, most of them unknown in

Europe, were practical and efficient and affected the entire system of labor relations as well as the economy. An old-age pension system, Social Security, was introduced. The National Labor Relations Act of 1935, also known as the Wagner Act, was the bill that secured full rights for unions and gave strength and the majesty of law to labor relations.

General welfare and expanded social legislation changed the conditions of working people and paved the way toward the further growth and development of labor rights. Roosevelt's administration left a rich heritage of social progress and advanced labor legislation.[64]

The Scandinavian countries, with Sweden at the helm, advanced a new kind of benevolent and protective state. The Scandinavian nations became the model of the "welfare state."

The British milestone that marked the general acceptance of social responsibilities by that state was called popularly the "Beveridge Plan." It was a 1942 report by Sir William Beveridge titled *Social Insurance and Allied Services* and was a bold postwar plan prepared by the British "Inter-departmental Committee on Social Insurance and Allied Services, charged to survey the existing national schemes of social insurance and allied services and to make recommendations."

The plan covered all citizens, "but had regard to their different ways of life," and made recommendations concerning a comprehensive social insurance system, embracing compensation for unemployment and disability, pension on retirement, medical treatment and funeral expenses. The Beveridge Plan—an extensive volume—was a part of a plan for peace in time of war, part of a postwar reconstruction project. The report initiated major social reforms in Britain.[65]

The Beveridge Plan was a landmark example for the British social history and social reform movement. It was also a major turning point in the history of labor legislation. Now the welfare state intervened into free market play in order to secure three objectives: minimum income, reduction or abolishment of economic insecurity and assurance "that all citizens [were] offered the best available social services."[66]

By the middle of the twentieth century the welfare state had wide public approval and acceptance. Social legislation entered the law books of almost all democratic, industrialized countries. A number of institutions and businesses implemented and enforced these laws and large sections of the nations enjoyed the benefits. It won support and approval as an integral part of democratic creed. Even the conservative economist and philosopher F. A. von Hayek, who was leading opponent of the extension of state powers (especially of economic interference of the state with the working of economic forces), accepted—in a limited form—the welfare state as an answer to some social problems: "There is the important issue of security, of protection against risks common to all, where government can often either reduce these risks or assist people to provide against them." Then he continued in favor of a "limited welfare state"—"a limited security, which in a free society can be achieved by all."⁶⁷

During the last decades of the twentieth century, the welfare state has come under strong criticism. It was argued that services went too far and affected the cost of production. In a global economy, it resulted in unemployment and other problems of advanced industrial nations, due to increased competition from developing nations, which have low wages and are not burdened by social services.

Whatever the arguments, a new problem appeared—or so it seemed—the problem of limits—how far the state could go with its assistance under current economic conditions. Moreover, a second issue arose: "what should be done" to cope with social problems for which public intervention thus far had not been effective.

In addition, the issue of limits for social assistance is accompanied by historical opposition to the extension of the powers of the state. Extension of the functions of the civic state into the wide social area has, however, fundamental causes. Due to economic changes, many vital functions shifted from the family and traditional associations to the state. In most cases, public assistance for those who need it is imperative for the very existence of a workable democratic nation; it is also one of its functions and missions.

Strengthening and protection of the family is of vital importance. Moreover, efforts have been made and should be explored to shift some social services to voluntary associations, financed in part from public revenues. This, however, depends on the strength and vitality of the civic society; expansive state intervention in the vast area of social legislation is imperative today. It is a corrective of social injustice, a control of exploitation.

The welfare state will not disappear. In fact, it continues in a reformed, adjusted way. It is the result of a long historical development, not solely from a few legislative acts; it is today part of our world outlook. It is also a working model of a benevolent democratic state, not a utopian one. It is not perfect, but it is thus far perhaps the best state man has been able to create, the best in terms of our ethics and efficient governments. It is not however an end station.

In a multiethnic democratic state, the extension of social services creates a strong bond. It reinforces the civic social-political identity. All those rights, social rights being broader than ethnic rights, are related—in a democratic state—to all citizens, irrespective of their ethnic origin, culture or religion.

What does this historical change mean in terms of defining of citizenship? Now, the social rights of the citizen have become an integral part of the definition of citizenship, at least for democratic nations of the world. Thus, the very concept has been broadened and redefined.

The redefinition of the concept of citizenship is not accidental. It is a necessary social corrective during times of rapid social-economic change, as well as a change toward the integration of states and nations into regional and global associations with a simultaneous tendency toward ethnic identification and preservation of ethnic cultures. It is a fitting and mature institution in construction of modern democratic multiethnic states. It calls, however, for a complementary effort in redefining and also accepting the corresponding duties and responsibilities by citizens, a condition of an efficient and well-working democratic state. This advanced form of modern citizenship is only an articulation of democratic forms of government and political culture.

Thus the modern, democratic citizenship is not solely of Greek and Roman vintage. True, the Greeks and Romans introduced the concept; in a sense they invented it. Particularly the Romans applied it in building a multiethnic, continental state, a state of free citizens, but still in a society based on slave economy. Medieval Italian and later other European continental cities inherited this institution and secured its continuation through the next ages. The English and British philosophers contributed the fundamental content based on principles of liberty and individual, human, civil and political rights. The French Revolution created the folklore, ideology, perhaps even a social myth, of the very term "citizen." The revolution fathered its worldwide appeal. The United States, after this long development, gave this institution modern meaning as an expression of equality of opportunities, personal freedom for all in a multiethnic and democratic state, second only to Rome when compared in political skills, to construct a multiethnic and wide continental state by means of this institution. International labor movement and the welfare state extended the definition of citizenship making it even broader and more humane by inclusion of social rights. It took two and a half millennia to develop and fully define this modern and widely accepted institution; it is also an articulation of our world outlook, profound changes of our society and political culture.

The modern democratic state and citizenship are the fruits of a long and painful history. It is not a system born of a single political act, reduced to one historical date. It is the creation of many generations, and it is now becoming a common shared heritage as well as a responsibility.

Democracy is a complex and difficult form of government rooted in theory and experience. To be successful it calls for enlightened and educated leadership and voters. Since it is a government by consent, its functioning depends on the active support of critical sections of the electorate. By "critical," we mean large and influential enough to make such a system a workable one.

In a multiethnic state, support for this polity and sentiments of allegiance and identity need to be shared by a variety of ethnic, cultural and religious groups. Hence, they must have and also recognize and support its efficient and successful functioning.

NOTES

1. Peter Riesenberg, *Citizenship in the Western Tradition: From Plato to Rousseau* (Chapel Hill: University of North Carolina Press, 1992), pp. 229, 260ff.

2. Ibid., pp. 95ff. and 198ff., 203.

3. Ibid., p. 220ff.

4. See the comprehensive and highly informative study by Pierre Rétat, "Citoyen-Sujet, Civisme," in Rolf Reinchardt and Ebenhart Schmitt, UPs., in association with Gerd Van Den Heuvel and Anette Hofer, *Handbuch Politisch—Sozialer Grundbegriffe in Frankreic 1680–1820* (Munich: K. Oldenburg, 1988), Heft 9. The text of the following dictionaries is quoted: Richelet, *Dictionnaire* (1680), Lyon 1728 edition (with additions of P. Aubert); Bodin, *Six Livres de la Republique* (1576); Puget, *Dictionnaire de Nations Primitives* (1773); all quotes from Rétat as above, p. 78ff.

5. J. J. Rousseau, *Du Contract Social* (1762; reprint. Paris: Bezat, n.d.), p. 26, n. 1, to chapter 6 (Du pact social).

6. Rétat, "Citoyen-Sujet, Civism," p. 76.

7. Montesquieu, *De L'Esprit des Lois* (1743; reprint. Paris: Garnier Freres, 1961), vol. 1, livre II, chapters 1 and 2, p. 11ff., and p. 29, livre V, chapter 3.

8. Paul H. D. Baron de Holbach, *Politique Naturelle* (London: N.p., 1773), quoted by Rétat, "Citoyen-Sujet, Civisme," p. 86ff. For an extensive and detailed study of the origin of French citizenship see, in addition to Rétat, as quoted, Renée Waldinger, Philip Dawson and Isser Woloch, eds., *French Revolution and the Meaning of Citizenship* (Westport, Conn.: Greenwood Press, 1993).

9. Rétat, "Citoyen-Sujet, Civisme," p. 83ff.

10. For a full discussion of the beginnings of the modern concept of citizenship in France see Waldinger, Dawson and Woloch, *French Revolution*, esp. Part I, "Toward New Conception of Citizenship," and chapters by Pierre Rétat, Madelyn Gurwitz, Michael P. Fitsimmons, Marriet B. Applewhite, Antoine de Barque and Marion A. Carlson.

11. See the chapter by Michael P. Fitsimmons, "The National Assembly and the Invention of Citizenship," in Waldinger, Dawson and Woloch, *French Revolution*, p. 29ff.

12. Rétat, "Citoyen-Sujet, Civisme," p. 90. For a penetrating analysis of the essay by Siéyès and its relevance see Mauro Barberis, "L'Ombra

Dello Stato. Siéyèes e le Origini Revoluzionarie dell' Idea di Nazione," *Il Politico*, no. 3 of (July–August–September 1991): 509ff.

13. Fitsimmons, "The National Assembly," p. 29ff., and also Introduction, p. xvi.

14. For early and detailed account of the process of change see M. A. Thiers, *The History of The French Revolution*, vol. 1 (London: Richard Bentley, 1836), p. 75ff.

15. On clubs and discussions see Gaetano Salvemini, *La Rivoluzione Francese* (Milan: Fetrinelli, 1964), p. 37. The Jacobin Clubs spread all over France, see Clarence Crane Brinton, *The Jacobins* (New York: Macmillan, 1930).

16. Jeremy D. Popkin, "Citizenship and the Press in the French Revolution," and Rétat, "The Revolution of Citizenship from the Ancien Regime to The Revolution," in Waldinger, Dawson and Woloch, *French Revolution*, pp. 123–36, 3–28.

17. Thiers, *History of the French Revolution*, p. 76ff.

18. See Marvin Carlson, "The Citizen in the Theater," Isser Woloch, "The Right to Primary Education in the French Revolution: From Theory to Practice," and Antoine de Barque, "The Citizen in Caricature," in Waldinger, Dawson and Woloch, *French Revolution*, pp. 81–88, 137–52, 59–80.

19. Quoted in Rétat, "Citoyen-Sujet, Civisme," p. 99; also nn. 56 and 57.

20. Joseph de Maistre, *Considerations* (1776), "Dans les gouvernment absolus et dans les monarchies tempérées, il n'y'a pas des citoyens, mais des sujets," quoted by Rétat, "Citoyen-Sujet, Civisme," pp. 103–4.

21. Madelyn Gurwitz, "Citoyen, Citoyennes: Cultural Regression and the Subversion of the French Revolution," and Darline G. Levy, "Women's Revolutionary Citizenship in Action," in Waldinger, Dawson and Woloch, *French Revolution*, pp. 17–28, 169–84.

22. "Discours de M. Le Comte De Mirabeau au nom Du Comiteè de Cinq." Text of his introduction to Declaration of the Rights of Man and Citizen in 1789, reprinted in Otis E. Fellows and Norman L. Torrey, eds., *The Age of Enlightenment—An Anthology* (New York: Appleton Century, Crofts, 1942), p. 635ff.

23. See Fitsimmons, "The National Assembly," p. 29.

24. On the American influence on the French Revolution see A. Aulard, *Etudes et Leçons sur la Revolution* (Paris: Alcan, 1921), p. 58ff.

25. Fernand Braudel, *The Identity of France* (New York: Harper & Row, 1988), p. 91ff.

26. A. Barruel, *Memoirs pour Servir a l'Histoire du Jacobinisme* (Hamburg: Fauche, 1798–99), quoted by Barberis, "L'Ombra Dello State," p. 510, n. 3.

27. J. B. McMaster, *A History of the People of the United States* (1895), as

quoted by M. (Moisei) Ostrogorski, *La Democratie et L' Organization de Partis Politiques*, vol. 1 (Paris: Calman Levy, 1905), p. 114.

28. John Richard Green, *A Short History of the English People* (New York: Harper & Brothers, 1890), p. 194.

29. Ibid., pp. 195–96.

30. George Macauley Trevelyan, *History of England* (London and New York: Longmans, Green & Co., 1937), p. 157ff.

31. Ibid., p. 192ff.

32. Ibid., p. 255.

33. See Raphael Sealey, *The Athenian Republic: Democracy or Rule of Law?* (University Park: Pennsylvania State University Press, 1987), p. 146ff.

34. John E. E. D. Acton, *Essays on Freedom and Power*. Edited with an Introduction by Gertrude Himmelfarb (Boston: Beacon, 1949).

35. Trevelyan, *History of England*, p. 157ff.

36. Courtney Ibert, *Parliament: Its History, Constitution and Practice* (London: Thornton Butterworth, 1932), p. 18ff.

37. J. A. Gierowski, *Historia Polski*, vol. 1. (Warszawa: P.W.N., 1982), pp. 59–63. With all its faults, the Polish republic of the nobles secured for a time a rule of religious tolerance, particularly in the sixteenth and seventeenth centuries. In the sixteenth and seventeenth centuries Poland became a haven for Unitarians (also known here as Aryans or Polish Brethren). (For a comprehensive and informative account of Polish Unitarians, see Peter Brock, "The Polish Antitrinitarians," *Pacifism in Europe* [Princeton, N.J.: Princeton University Press, 1972], pp. 114–61.) The Polish Lithuanian Commonwealth was at that time a major center and refuge for Socinians. Since Protestantism has been enhanced by segments of the nobility, they were not eager to empower an otherwise weak Polish Inquisition. The situation changed, however, toward the end of the seventeenth and eighteenth centuries. See also: George H. Williams, *The Polish Brethren, Documents and Thoughts of Unitarians* in "The Polish-Lithuanian Commonwealth, 1601–1685," *Harvard Theological Studies* 30 (1980); Stanislaw Kot, *Ideologia Polityczna i Spoleczna Braci Polskich, Zwanych Aryanami* (Political and social ideology of Polish brethren, called Aryans) (Warszawa: Kasa Mianowskiego, 1931), (in Polish); Z. Koriyanowa, *Bracia Polscy* (Polish brethren) (Warszawa: Warszawakie Tow. Naukowe, 1929), (in Polish).

38. Mary Taylor Blauwelt, *The Development of Cabinet Government in England* (New York: Macmillan, 1908), p. 148ff.

39. F. C. Montague, *The Elements of English Constitutional History* (London and New York: Longmans, Green & Co., 1908), p. 148ff.

40. Paul Miliukov, *Outlines of Russian Culture* (Philadelphia: University of Pennsylvania Press, 1948), p. vii.

41. James H. Kettner, *The Development of American Citizenship, 1608–1870* (Chapel Hill: University of North Carolina Press, 1978), p. 7ff.

42. Ibid., pp. 9–11.

43. Ibid., p. 9.

44. Ibid., p. 61.

45. Ibid., pp. 73–75, 84–86, 242ff., 326ff., 340–44.

46. Ibid., pp. 61ff., 343ff., 348.

47. Herman Belz, *Emancipation and Equal Rights* (New York: Norton, 1978), p. 129ff., esp. chapter 5, "Nationalization of Civil Rights," pp. 108–50.

48. Don E. Ferenbacher, *Slavery Law and Politics. The Dred Scott Case in Historical Perspective* (Oxford: Oxford University Press, 1988). The literature on American citizenship is extensive; a few monographs are mentioned here just as examples. See Judith Sklar, *The American Citizenship: The Quest for Inclusion* (Boston: Harvard University Press, 1991); Luella Gettys, *The Law of Citizenship in the United States* (Chicago: The University of Chicago Press, 1934). However, James H. Kettner's comprehensive volume covers major historical issues of this key American political institution and gives an excellent critical survey of its development.

49. Roger Brubaker, *Citizenship and Nationhood in France and Germany* (Boston: Harvard University Press, 1992).

50. Alexis de Tocqueville, *The Old Regime and the French Revolution* (Garden City, N.Y.: Doubleday, 1955), p. 43.

51. Brubaker, *Citizenship and Nationhood*, p. 194.

52. Ibid., pp. 103, 106; also, Introduction, p. x.

53. Germany has a variety of categories for foreigners, listed and discussed by Manfred Kuechler in his informative paper presented at the Annual Meeting of the American Political Science Association (APSA) in 1993, and also at the 1994 conference of the CUNY Academy for Humanities and Sciences: Manfred Kuechler, "The Germans and The Others: Racism, Xenophobia, or Self-defense," 1993 Annual Meeting of the APSA. Manuscript copy courtesy of the author.

54. Brubaker, *Citizenship and Nationhood*, pp. 77ff., 81ff.; also, Kuechler.

55. Reinhard Bendix, *Nation-Building and Citizenship* (Berkeley: University of California Press, 1977), p. 91ff.; T. H. Marshall, *Citizenship and Social Development* (Garden City, N.Y.: Doubleday, 1964), p. 91ff.

56. In 1943 this writer suggested pinternationalization of social security systems in Europe, especially for health and retirement, as a way to create a strong transnational European bond and weaken nationalist tendencies. This would have also created a stronger and more advanced social security system especially in Central Eastern Europe. See Feliks Gross, "Internationalization of Social Insurance," *Left News* (London) 84 (June 1943).

57. Arnold Toynbee, *The Industrial Revolution* (1882; reprint, Boston: Beacon Press, 1957), p. 66.

58. Ibid., p. 61.

59. Lois Le Chapelier, speech reprinted in *Freedom of Association* (ILO Studies and Reports, Series A, no. 28, London: King & Son, 1928), p. 11, reprinted in Bendix, *Nation-Building and Citizenship*, p. 101.

60. Harry W. Laidler, *History of Socialism* (New York: Thomas Y. Crowell, 1968), p. 60ff.

61. Lorenz von den Stein, *The History of Social Movements in France, 1789–1850* (1850; reprint Totowa, N.J.: Bedminster Press, 1964), pp. 382–93, 397ff., 422ff.

62. Laidler, *History of Socialism*, p. 738ff.

63. F. Engels, *The Conditions of the Working Class in England* (New York: Macmillan, 1958), p. x, Appendix III, "Preface to the English Edition of 1892," p. 360.

64. Paul K. Conkin, *F.D.R. and the Origins of the Welfare State* (New York: Thomas Y. Crowell, 1967), p. 62ff. Also, Sidney Fine, *Laissez Faire and the General Welfare State* (Ann Arbor: University of Michigan Press, 1967), and Charles L. Schottland, ed., *The Welfare State* (New York: Harper & Row, 1967).

65. William Beveridge, *Social Insurance and Allied Services* (New York: Macmillan, 1942).

66. Asa Briggs, "The Welfare State in Historical Perspective," in Schottland, *The Welfare State*, pp. 17, 25ff.

67. Friedrich von Hayek, "The Decline of Socialism and the Rise of the Welfare State," in Schottland, *The Welfare State*, p. 241.

5

CONCLUDING COMMENTS

I

Institutions by themselves do not make a good or bad polity, a workable or disorganized state. Institutions are an important, even necessary system of structures, but not a sufficient one. People who manage institutions are an essential part of them. Their quality makes the institutions desirable and beneficial; it is not just the organization or the structure that determines its success or failure. In simple words, institutions are as good as the citizens who run them. Moreover, the same institutions can be used and misused in a variety of ways.

Once laws and effective institutions have been assimilated into the general political culture, they affect social and political behavior, reinforce values and with time create traditions, lore, even symbolism and rituals. Once a democratic civic state has been accepted and put into practice by the citizenry of a civil society, it will humanize society, set limits to the use of force and build a system of civic controls over the centers of political and economic power.

The civic state is not a "perfect" state, an "ideal" one, a "utopia," but a working and humane system, and its merits should be recognized especially when compared to other systems of goverment throughout our long history. The cruelty displayed by rulers of powerful and once highly advanced states should also make us aware of other brutal alternatives and the ambivalent nature of man and the frightening potentialities of the human race.

Slavery, once banned by advanced nations, returned to Europe and Asia with Hitler, Stalin and Mao and was politely ignored by diplomats and confused or timid intellectuals. Those regimes also moved along one of mankind's historical roads, which they had chosen as a historical option. When reviewing the chronicles of history, we rediscover again and again the long chain of cruelty afflicted by man to man, a chain of ages and millennia, where cruelty was rationalized at times by religions and powerful religious hierarchies and later by ideologies and political leadership.

But, there was another historical road that was also open to mankind which included the history of state building and actions of free men who set this direction and paved the way toward a benevolent polity. Hence it is proper, even necessary, to remember that it took centuries to develop the civic and benevolent polity that many of us live in; citizenship is its major symbol and institution.

II

This simple verity is again relevant during times of rapid social change, presently prompted by technological advances. Social change affects of course the state and our institutions. Institutions and political systems have to be adjusted to new realities. Moreover, responsible government exercises reasonable controls and sets necessary safeguards to prevent negative effects resulting from rapid change.

Even during a revolution not "everything" has to be changed; moreover, such a total change may prompt anarchy and man-made disasters, which in the past, ended more often than not in dictatorships and oppressive rule.

An enlightened view is open not solely to change, but also considers the human and material cost, the need for stability, hence problems of continuity and conservation; in consequence the conservative side of the issue has to be considered. A distinction has to be made between those norms and institutions that should be not weakened or changed—thus should be conserved—from those subject to change and even radical abolition. Enlightened and rational leadership distinguishes between what should be conserved from what should be changed.

The very fact that an institution is old, or even ancient, does not make it necessarily useless or bad. To the contrary, such an institution or norm may be essential or workable and its preservation, even reinforcement, may be vital for the welfare of large sections of citizens.

There are of course institutions that are oppressive and have to be removed and others that secure freedom and should be strengthened. The French Revolution abolished the Inquisition and a code of oppressive laws, but Jacobin leaders, in their zeal of extreme factionalism, tried to change everything and destroy all vestiges of the past through the use of violence and terror. The problem was not only of change, which was needed, but also what to change and how to change.

Change and stability are not necessarily contradictory. A powerful historical change of views, philosophies, world outlook—but above all in the areas of economics and technology—calls for strong institutions that are able to channel the social process of change in an orderly, peaceful and nonviolent manner in order to secure stability.

Rapid social change that avoids disintegration and anarchy calls for retaining some basic institutions of stability. Civic institutions belong here. They are rooted in our basic values, the core values of our culture. Our culture indeed is built on many values that secure continuity. Any weakening of these values may affect the entire political as well as cultural edifice. Our institutions of civil and human rights, our institutions of freedom, belong here. They are indeed the core of a widely shared political creed.

These values, as well as institutions, have universal appeal, affect the entire industrialized world and are the product of and at the root of our civilization. They are recognized universally and stated today in the United Nations Declaration of Human Rights as well as in the entire system of international legislation (conventions).

To this arena also belongs the view of humanity as a unity, the recognition of equal rights for all members of humankind and respect for cultural differences, religion or creed.

There is today, however, a strong, and at times violent, trend of opposition and protest against the principles that are deeply rooted in Western civilization, where they have also matured and were institutionalized. The fundamentalist Islamic movement opposes even equal rights for women, expels them from schools and professions in Afghanistan, forces them to wear chadors or veils in Iran and Afghanistan and prohibits the enjoyment of music.

Anti-Western trends also appeared on American college campuses. Some students and faculty members opposed the dominance of Western history or humanities in university curricula. Non-Western nations and civilizations, their contributions and historical roles should of course be studied and taught as part of many academic programs, and in fact they are. Interest in different, non-European cultures is strong—above all—in the West, and studies in this area appeared early on at universities because it is a civilization that is universal in its very nature (and the universal viewpoint and world outlook are also a part of it).

Indeed, it is thanks to this Western culture, that equal rights are extended to all, irrespective of ethnicity or religion, and it is citizenship that protects the equal rights of all. It is also this civilization that moves by fusion and exchange with other cultures toward a universal civilization, shared by many all over the globe. It is an inclusive civilization that favors diversity and continuity of all cultures, an open culture as opposed to narrow, exclusive creeds.

III

Our current technological change is unusually rapid and, at the same time, perilous and full of risks. Powerful forces, energies, have been released before mankind has learned how to control them adequately. On the other hand however, science, next to the humanities contributes to an emergence of an extensive universal civilization, as well as to the growth of a global economy that affects almost all of mankind. It is a powerful historical trend, that may or may not slow down or even change. When we look back, such was the fate of Greek culture or the Renaissance. Those were indeed relatively short historical periods of intellectual and artistic flourish in almost every field. But now, the process seems to accelerate.

In such a period of rapid change, even more than in times when tradition prevailed or change was slow, the strength of our institutions and of civil society, of basic and voluntary social institutions and associations is vital. They are vital in providing continuity and an additional social safety net as technology affects us strongly and changes our ways of life as well as the immediate environment of urban and rural existence.

The civic state, unlike the totalitarian state, is limited in its functions. Its effectiveness and success depends on the proper balance between the civil society and the state. The state, however, cannot meet all of of our needs, especially in the area of personal relationships and support. Our sentiments and emotions are the part of our lives associated, above all, with what a Greek philosopher would call natural primary bonds, hence family, or our cultural or nationality groups, as well as bonds of religion or shared philosophy or ideology, tradition, lore and sentiments, which are also vital to our sense of belonging.

In a well-working democratic state, ethnic diversity is a source of strength, cultural wealth and creativity. These are also some of the essential bonds within the civic society. In times of personal or family crisis or catastrophe, here is an important, even if additional source of direct assistance, as well as emotional refuge, that cannot be replaced by public institutions.

Today, with many states of large immigrant populations the ethnic bond is particularly important for new-comers and first generations. Later, with the third generation, the process of assimilation, more often than not weakens the ethnic bonds, which are displaced by new vital associations.

Many of those primary and basic associations, particularly family and kinship, were indeed affected by powerful economic and technological changes; the natural bonds grew often weaker. Public institutions took over some of the functions once in hands of the family or simply neighborhood groups. Oftentimes this was and is to the greater benefit of those who needed assistance and not to their detriment.

Nevertheless, continuity and strength of this entire network of basic and voluntary groups, associations, neighborhoods and communities is even more vital today during times of rapid change and ensuing pressures as a result of powerful social trends and technological changes. Their strength again secures flexibility and ability of adjustment in times of substantial transformation of our living conditions. The weakening or even disappearance of some of these bonds may result in an emotional void and alienation.

There are also other developments that point to the need and reinforcement for primary and voluntary bonds that give us a particular economic, social, emotional, as well as personal, shelter. Here belongs the emergence of the enormous economic power of large corporations. Economic power centers have been created that are not subject to a democratic process, where executive power has wide economic power and can range free from any checks and balances, save the public control of the state and strong labor unions and political parties led by honest committed people.

In a free market, unrestrained by law and ethical imperatives, the fate of thousands depends on temporary gains, the profit of the few. The profit motive is far stronger than the public interest and is the driving force behind the market—and it works. In a long-range perspective, however, it works, but in many cases it hurts and hurts badly, and may even hurt "totally," to a point of a calamity.

Our environment is deteriorating at a very rapid pace; clean air and clean water are urgent priorities today. Our protective forest ranges are subject to rapid depletion, particularly in those areas where public interest groups and the state are unable or unwilling to intervene and act prudently and rationally, especially in terms of impact and carefully considered actions and plans.

The strong balance of social and political power is imperative to remedy and counter the negative effects of our booming age that may end in a crisis, even in a man-made disaster that could have been avoided. On one hand there appears a need for public action, and good, rational and humane government, and on the other there is a need for strong voluntary associations, for a wide range of public interest groups, political parties and labor unions that defend the interests of those who do not share the benefits of growing wealth and contrariwise, are harmed by the rapid growth. Growing and influential public interest associations affect public opinion in those matters of general welfare and environment.

Problems that loom in a long-range perspective are indeed immense. Public intervention of the state next to private agencies and planning in many areas is imperative. Planning has been compromised by communist and totalitarian regimes. But planning continues to be vital in many areas; and in the future it will increase.

Future development, environmental difficulties and economic welfare are problem areas that will increase, not diminish, the areas of activities of the state and international bodies. Hence, the voluntary civic segment is essential to strengthening the civil society in providing a proper balance between those realms.

The civic state per se does not suggest a general answer to all those problems. The state and particularly the civic state is a structure, a complex set of institutions. True, it provides a proper instrument to channel change into nonviolent, peaceful and humane policies. It is a good instrumentality in hands of good, intelligent and competent people. But, it can also be used for a variety of other not so well-meaning objectives.

IV

This powerful tendency toward a global economy, cannot be arrested and reaches the most distant, even isolated, corners of the world. It depends to a large extent on our wisdom whether its impact will be benevolent or harmful. It will also affect the problem of nationality and the very meaning of ethnicity, its definition and changing nature. Not only will scientists, scholars, artists or writers, and people in many professions and endeavors live within this global universal civilization; it is already upon us and is increasing in its profusion and significance.

In the future, this will become even more universal and "common" although people will not realize it and may not perceive in this way. We are learning to live within not just one single culture, but two or more cultures. Telecommunication is only one major aspect of change. The global universal aspects of our civilization, are broad, immense. The ethnic community as a nation, as a traditional community of common culture, often common, historical suffering, shared sentiments and relationships, folklore and vitality, continues to be for many a home, a roof that shelters cultural vitality and continuity.

It remains and will continue in its vitality, rooted in native languages and cultural vicinity. Weaker, smaller, ethnic groupings, not only in a multinational state, but also in all parts of the globe, will need protection against adversities and some of the more powerful and agressive groups. In a multinational state thus far, in a democracy, the ancient institution of citizenship extends its protective shield over minorities and ethnic groups but, above all, over the human and political rights of all. Not unlike the history of religious freedom, the distinction and separation of the state and ethnicity is the way to free, nonviolent development and growth.

Thus far, taking a long historical perspective, a democratic civic state offered freedom and conditions of growth for a variety of nationalities throughout a long history of conquest and persecutions that marked the road, a major road, of the history of mankind. Citizenship is a protective institution of the weaker. The civic state offered thus far, a humane and constructive answer to the dilemmas of a multiethnic state. It also provided peaceful avenues of improvement and change. Moreover, it is still a working plan. It must be repeated: This is not the only plan. There are also alternatives and variations as well as new innovative approaches. Tradition and culture may call for different answers that still protect the basic rights of a person. Part of our definition of a humane and benevolent state is the reluctance to impose, to force, an a priori "ready made" political system.

It is good to look back and search the history of major institutions, to remember the past not only for freedom, but also for oppression and suffering. Then, we may say simply: This is a good, working polity.

Criticism is—and rightly so—part of our world-view. However, criticism that disregards or misinterprets merits, is like a road sign that points to a wrong direction. As we search for a policy along the historical road that extends beyond problems of today, even beyond a single generation, it is not to keep in mind a vision of a perfect state or a perfect institution. We should not underestimate the function and significance of our need for a vision, which is the need of a creative imagination. But to be able to envision and imagine alternatives and select a preferred option is an essential part of any problem solving.

Any attempt or plan to improve society, to build a better state, a more humane community, calls for a vision, even a distant one, and includes a remote image that sets the direction of our goals and pragmatic targets, generates actions and invigorates our efforts. A vision of a future state or society might have its own beauty and logical sense. It might even be poetic. These qualities, however, are far from sufficient should we search for a working practical answer rather than the abstract ideal of a perfect solution.

Another way we gain insight and a corrective outlook is by also looking in a different direction, not solely forward to the unknown future, but also at past experiences, at ways man has been successful, and that in the past have led to the achievement of set goals and have paved the way toward a more caring society. True, each new situation may call for entirely new, original and daring responses to the challenge. Past experience, however, assists our judgment and suggests answers and alternatives that are perhaps not as beautiful and poetic as a vision of an ideal perfect society, perfect in logic and harmony. From the past we may also discover errors and faults that might have been responsible for failures.

Thus, in our effort to find solutions for the present we need to examine and understand the past. From the past we may discover what worked and gave a beneficent result and what did not work and resulted harmful solutions. The roots of a democratic society, its meaning, can be found by examining and probing its strong and weak attributes. The historical road signs are there, as well as the essential values that guide its policies.

The democratic concept of citizenship embodies the essentials of democracy. Democracy is not solely a form of a government, particularly one based on assemblies. This is not a sufficient definition of what democracy meant for many and what is understood today by this term. Reduced to its very essence, democracy is a creed, a faith of the inalienable rights of man, of a person, of every person. These rights shelter the corresponding tenets of personal individual freedom and commitment to assume responsibilities. They form the very roots of democracy.

In this sense theories of natural law and social contract are valid, although in terms of empirical, historical data they are wrong. They are valid "a priori," as a principle derived from ethical and political imperatives, the fruit of rational considerations and reason. This is of course not a literal acceptance of ancient theory, but a reinterpretation.

The electoral format or practice, simply as a way of securing illusory legitimacy is of course not sufficient evidence of a democratic state or government. Past and contemporary governments of oppression and discrimination, also totalitarian governments, were more often than not, legitimizing their authority by subservient councils they called parliaments, soviets, fascist councils or theocratic assemblies. Even assemblies elected by a majority vote, unless respectful of individual rights and rights of minorities are not necessarily democratic in the sense of tradition and history. By "historical" we mean here the way it has been defined on a historical road to freedom and political rights by those who carried the ideas and paved the road toward a democratic form of government. This was also one of the historical roads mankind has trod, one guided by a vision of a gentle, humane and just society, free from oppression and cruelty, in contrast to the "other" road of "glory," conquest and oppression.

Democracy as a form of government is tantamount to a state of a free citizen operating under the rule of law. Tyrannies, whether those of the majority or minority, have no respect for elementary human rights. Individual rights, as well as political, civil and elementary human rights, are the test and measure of a democratic government, not just institutional structures.

No state is a perfect one, hence citizenship even in a well-working, efficient democratic state is the ultimate shelter of an individual. Citizenship is indeed the shield of a free man and guardian of his dignity and rights.

Prejudice however cannot be eliminated fully simply by decree or government policy. Even a fully adequate, strong equal rights policy of an efficient and consistent democratic government cannot eliminate deep, rationalized and traditional prejudices. Experience teaches that, in long run, public policies that are consistent and that have been practiced for many decades (especially judicial decisions) have their beneficial effects and affect the views and attitudes of many.

A further, perhaps deeper modification of views, attitudes and values of general behavior calls for broader and more in-depth action within the civil society. It calls above all for wide educational programs and efforts, community action and other projects. Such programs involve communities and private voluntary associations and neighborhood programs. Many cities in the United States were quite effective in controlling, or at least lowering, racial and ethnic barriers. This does not mean that prejudices and deeply rooted sentiments, nor inveterate antagonisms were entirely eradicated. Nevertheless, after decades of effort progress has been evident, noticeable in everyday business and human relations.

Advances have also been made in understanding ethnic problems and relations, in understanding the nature of prejudice. Scholarship in this area is extensive indeed (to mention only from the vast area of literature on this subject an early and important work of Gordon Allport and Gardner Murphy). No doubt, citizenship in many civic states has its social and educational "base," a necessary support "from below," a kind of informal social "infrastructure." Laws alone and government policies are not sufficient.

Effective citizenship as a key institution of a multiethnic state also calls for actions and efforts of the minorities, of the ethnic groups not solely from the majority nation. In a multicultural society and state, adjustment has to be made by both: by the established majorities but also by the immigrant ethnic minorities. It is a kind of social "domestication." The level of difference has to be lowered and cultural adjustment made by the immigrant ethnic group. Some immigrant customs and practices might be incompatible with the institutions and culture of the host nation (e.g., polygamy, low status of women, use of violence in the political process).

Citizenship is a kind of "superstructure." Its meaning and effectiveness in everyday practice is derived from the entire political culture. It is, after all, an articulation of the civic state and an expression of its nature, functions and practices.

It seems to me that we still need to know more about the nature of difference: why certain types of distinctions may trigger hostility (which may have, of course, far deeper roots) and why other types of distinctions are easier to accept. In medieval times ethnic differences were easier to accept than religious discrepancies (as evidenced in the practical life in medieval cities). Today in the Islamic world, ethnic differences may be accepted by the fundamentalist, but not differences of a religious or sectarian nature.

There is still a long way to go. We may never reach a state where prejudice has been eliminated completely. We are simply human and not perfect. Although beyond the understanding of reasonable people, some abhorrence of cultural traits, some strong likes and dislikes, will of course continue. Some people may have a rational explanation for this, while others may not, with reasons hidden deep in their emotional psyches, next to their hostilities and aggressive tendencies.

Nevertheless, as we have already learned, change is possible, a change toward the basic improvement of human relations and the elimination of discrimination, diminishing and, in some cases, perhaps, eradicating prejudice.

The advance toward a more humane and more benign humanity has begun. Effective citizenship in a multiethnic state is a major expression of this trend, a signpost on this road.

SELECTED
BIBLIOGRAPHY

Acton, John E. E. D. *Essays on Freedom and Power*. Edited and introduction by Gertrude Himmelfarb. Boston: Beacon, 1949.

Alfoldy, Geza. *Social History of Rome*. Baltimore: Johns Hopkins University Press, 1987.

Althusius, Johannes. *The Politics of Johannes Althusius, Politica Methodice Digesta atque Exemplis et Profanis Illustrata*. Translated and introduction by Frederick Carney, preface by Carl J. Friedrich. (1603). Reprint, Boston: Beacon Press, 1964.

Aristotle. *The Politics of Aristotle*. Edited and translated by Ernest Barker. 1942. Reprint, London: Oxford University Press, 1965.

Aulard, A. *Etudes et Leçons sur la Revolution*. Paris: Alcan, 1921.

Bagehot, Walter. *The English Constitution*. London: Watts, 1967.

Bailey, Cyril, ed. *The Legacy of Rome*. 1923. Reprint, Oxford: Clarendon Press, 1962.

Barker, Ernest. *Essays on Government*. Oxford: Clarendon Press, 1946.

———. *Principles of Social and Political Theory*. London: Oxford University Press, 1967.

Belz, Herman. *Emancipation and Equal Rights*. New York: Norton, 1978.

Bendix, Reinhard. *Nation-Building and Citizenship*. Berkeley: University of California Press, 1977.

Beveridge, William. *Report on Social Insurance and Allied Services*. New York: Macmillan, 1942.

Blauwelt, Mary Taylor. *The Development of Cabinet Government in England*. New York: Macmillan, 1908.

Bloch, Marc. *Feudal Society*. Chicago: The University of Chicago Press, Vol. 1, 1970, Vol 2, 1971.

Bogdanor, Vernon. *The Monarchy and the Constitution*. London: Oxford University Press, 1995.

Braudel, Fernand. *The Identity of France*. New York: Harper & Row, 1988.

Briggs, Asa. "The Welfare State in Historical Perspective." In Charles L. Schottland, ed., *The Welfare State*. New York: Harper & Row, 1967.

Brubaker, Roger. *Citizenship and Nationhood in France and Germany*. Boston: Harvard University Press, 1992.

Burns, J. H., ed. *The Cambridge History of Medieval Political Thought*. Cambridge: Cambridge University Press, 1991.

Conkin, Paul K. *F.D.R. and the Origins of the Welfare State*. New York: Thomas Y. Crowell, 1967.

Coulanges, Fustel de. *La Cité Antique*. Paris: Librairie Hachette, n.d.

Crane Brinton, Clarence. *English Political Thought*. New York and Evanston, Ill.: Harper & Row, 1962.

Dahl, Robert A. *A Preface to Democratic Theory*. Chicago: The University of Chicago Press, 1956.

Engels, F. *The Conditions of the Working Class in England*. New York: Macmillan, 1958.

Fine, Sidney. *Laissez Faire and the General Welfare State*. Ann Arbor: University of Michigan Press, 1967.

Forenbacher, Don E. *Slavery, Law and Politics: The Dred Scott Case in Historical Perspective*. London: Oxford University Press, 1988.

Freedom of Association. ILO Studies and Reports, Series A, no. 28. London: King & Son, 1928.

Friedman, W. *Legal Theory*. London: Stevens, 1960.

Friedrich, Carl J., ed. *Totalitarianism*. New York: Universal Library, 1964.

Garin, Eugenio. *L'Umanismo Italiano*. Bari: Laterza, 1964.

———. *Scienza e Vita Civile nel Rinascimento Italiano*. Bari: Laterza, 1965.

Gettys, Luella. *The Law of Citizenship in the United States*. Chicago: The University of Chicago Press, 1934.

Gierke, Otto. *Natural Law and Theory of Society: 1500–1800*. Translated and introduction by Ernest Barker. 1930. Reprint, Boston: Beacon Press, 1957.

Grazia, Sebastian de. *The Political Community*. Chicago: The University of Chicago Press, 1948.

Green, John Richard. *A Short History of the English People*. New York: Harper & Brothers, 1890.

Hobbes, Thomas. *De Cive or The Citizen* (1642). Edited with an Introduction by Sterling P. Lamprecht. New York: Appleton Century & Crofts, 1949.

Ibert, Courtney. *Parliament: Its History, Constitution and Practice*. London: Thornton Butterworth, 1932.

Ihering, Rudolf von. "Entwicklungs Geschichte des Römischen Rechts." In Fritz Buchwald, ed., *Der Geist des Rechts. Ein Auswahl aus Seinen Schriften.* Bremen: Carl Schunemann Verlag, 1965.

Jones, A. H. M. *Athenian Democracy.* Baltimore: Johns Hopkins University Press, 1986.

Kettner, James T. *The Development of American Citizenship, 1608–1870.* Chapel Hill: University of North Carolina Press, 1978.

Krader, Lawrence. *Formation of the State.* Englewood Cliffs, N.J.: Prentice-Hall, 1968.

Laidler, Harry W. *History of Socialism.* New York: Thomas Y. Crowell, 1968.

Laski, Harold J. *A Grammar of Politics.* London: Allen and Unwin, 1928.

———. *Parliamentary Government in England.* New York: Viking, 1938.

———. *The State in Theory and Practice.* New York: Viking Press, 1968.

Leoni, Bruno. *Freedom and the Law.* Indianapolis: Liberty Fund, 1991.

Lewis, Ewart. *Medieval Political Ideas.* New York: Cooper Square Publishers, 1974.

Lintott, Andrew W. *The Constitution of the Roman Republic.* Oxford: Clarendon Press, 1999.

MacIver, R. M. *The Web of Government.* New York: Free Press, 1965.

McLennan, Gregor, David Held, and Stuart Hall, eds. *The Idea of Modern State.* Philadelphia: Open University, 1984.

Maine, Henry Sumner. *Ancient Law, Its Relation with the Early History of Society and Its Relation to Modern Society and Its Ideas.* 1861, 1863. Reprint, Boston: Beacon Press, 1963.

Maitland, F. W. *The Constitutional History of England.* Cambridge: Cambridge University Press, 1921.

Manville, Philip B. *The Origins of Citizenship in Ancient Athens.* Princeton, N.J.: Princeton University Press, 1990.

Marshall, T. H. *Citizenship and Social Development.* Garden City, N.Y.: Doubleday, 1964.

Marsilius of Padua. *The Defender of Peace (Defensor Pacis).* Translated and introduced by Alan Gewirth. 1956. Reprint, New York: Harper & Row, 1967. (Originally written in 1324.)

Mesnard, Pierre. *Il Pensiero Politico Rinascimentale.* 2 vols. French Edition, 1951. Bari: Laterza, 1965.

Millar, Fergus. *The Crowd in Rome in the Late Republic.* Ann Arbor: University of Michigan Press, 1998.

Mommsen, Theodor. *The History of Rome.* New York: Philosophical Library, n.d.

Montague, F. C. *The Elements of English Constitutional History.* London and New York: Longmans, Green & Co., 1908.

Montesquieu. *De L'Esprit des Lois.* 1743. Reprint, Paris: Garnier Freres, 1961.

Oldfield, Adrian. *Citizenship and Community*. London: Routledge, 1990.

Oppenheimer, Franz. *State*. Indianapolis: Bobbs-Merrill, 1914.

Pellicani, Luciano. *The Genesis of Capitalism and the Origins of Modernity*. New York: Telos, 1994.

Pirenne, Henri. *Economic and Social History of Medieval Europe*. New York: Harcourt, Brace, 1937.

————. *Medieval Cities*. 1925. Reprint, Garden City, N.Y.: Doubleday, 1956.

Poggi, Gianfranco. *The Development of the Modern State*. Stanford, Calif.: Stanford University Press, 1968.

Rétat, Pierre. "Citoyen-Sujet, Civisme." In Rolf Reinchardt and Ebenhart Schmitt, eds., *Verbindung mit Gerd Van Den Heuvel und Anette Hofer, Handbuch Politisch—Sozialer Grundbegriffe in Frankreic, 1680–1820*. Munich: K. Oldenburg, 1988.

Riesenberg, Peter. *Citizenship in the Western Tradition: From Plato to Rousseau*. Chapel Hill: University of North Carolina Press, 1992.

Rousseau, J. J. *Du Contract Social*. 1762. Reprint, Paris: Bezat, n.d.

Schlesinger, Arthur M., Jr. *Discovering America*. New York: Norton, 1992.

Schottland, Charles L., ed. *The Welfare State*. New York: Harper & Row, 1967.

Sealey, Raphael. *The Athenian Republic: Democracy or Rule of Law?* University Park: Pennsylvania State University Press, 1987.

Sherwin-White, A. N. *The Roman Citizenship*. London: Oxford University Press, 1987.

Sismondi, J. C. L. Sismonde de. *History of the Italian Republics*. Magnolia, Mass.: Peter Smith, 1970.

Sklar, Judith. *The American Citizenship: The Quest for Inclusion*. Boston: Harvard University Press, 1991.

Staley, Edgecumbe. *The Guilds of Florence*. 1906. Reprint, New York: Benjamin Bloom, 1967.

Stein, Lorenz von. *The History of Social Movements in France, 1789–1850*. 1850. Reprint, Totowa, N.J.: Bedminster Press, 1964.

Tivey, Leonard. *The Nation State*. New York: St. Martin's Press, 1981.

Trevelyan, George Macauley. *History of England*. London and New York: Longmans, Green & Co., 1937.

Waldinger, Renée, Philip Dawson, and Isser Woloch, eds. *French Revolution and the Meaning of Citizenship*. Westport, Conn.: Greenwood Press, 1993.

Weber, Max. *The City*. Glencoe, Ill.: Free Press, 1958.

Whitehead, David. *The Demes of Attica, 508–ca 250 B.C.* Princeton, N.J.: Princeton University Press, 1986.

Witt, Ronald G., with Elizabeth B. Welles, eds. *The Earthly Republic: Italian Humanists on Government and Society*. Philadelphia: University of Pennsylvania Press, 1978.

INDEX

About the Author

FELIKS GROSS is Professor Emeritus of Sociology at the Graduate School and Brooklyn College, City University of New York, honorary president of CUNY Academy for Humanities and Sciences. Professor Gross has published more than 14 books and numerous articles, primarily in political sociology.

ISBN 0-313-30932-9

90000>

EAN

9 780313 309328

HARDCOVER BAR CODE